MW01286803

estherpress

Books for Courageous Women

ESTHER PRESS VISION

Publishing diverse voices that encourage and equip women to walk courageously in the light of God's truth for such a time as this.

BIBLICAL STATEMENT OF PURPOSE

"For if you remain silent at this time, relief and deliverance for the Jews will arise from another place, but you and your father's family will perish. And who knows but that you have come to your royal position for such a time as this?"

– Esther 4:14

What people are saying about ...

BEING FULLY KNOWN

"*Being Fully Known* is a powerful guide for women who desire to connect with the truest parts of themselves while embracing the unshakable truth of God's love. Saundra beautifully weaves together Scripture, science, and personal experience to help readers shed false beliefs and pressures. Her words are both a mirror and a map—encouraging women to behold, become, and belong as they step fully into their God-given identities. This book is a breath of fresh air for those who feel overwhelmed and are ready to embrace the fullness of life that God intends. Highly recommended for those seeking both spiritual depth and personal transformation."

Marshawn Evans Daniels, Godfidence Coach®, TV personality, reinvention strategist for women, founder of SheProfits.com

"If your life feels like a whirlwind of striving yet lacks the joy and satisfaction that you thought would be yours by now, this book is for you. With deep wisdom and a compassionate voice, Dr. Saundra invites you into stillness and leads you to the true rest your soul craves. This book will help you move from doing to being, from unrest to flourishing, and from shallow connection to a deeply rooted relationship with God. Expect true life change in these pages!"

Jennifer Dukes Lee, author of *Growing Slow* and *It's All Under Control*

"*Being Fully Known* is full of heart and grounded wisdom on releasing the false identities we build around achievement. Dr. Saundra's words feel like a friend guiding me back to myself. This book is a gift for any woman who has ever felt worn down by expectations and shows a better way forward."

Alli Worthington, business coach, entrepreneur

"Dr. Saundra Dalton-Smith is the wise, compassionate, healing voice our world needs more than ever. Her words in *Being Fully Known* are more than helpful information; they're a soul-deep invitation out of hurry and into the presence of the God who longs to restore our weary hearts."

Holley Gerth, Wall Street Journal-bestselling author of *You're Already Amazing*

"I have read Dr. Saundra Dalton-Smith's books. I have heard her speak. I've interviewed her on my podcast. The result is always the same: She is accomplished and confident. Not just because of who she, but because of Whose she is. In her book, *Being Fully Known*, Dr. Dalton-Smith encourages me to find myself at the end of myself. She challenges me to step off the merry-go-round of competition and comparison to find my worth and value, not in doing it all but in being who Christ has made me to be. And that is being totally and completely His."

Babbie Mason, Dove Award-winning singer-songwriter and bestselling author of *Each One Reach One*

"Soul-searching. Life-giving. Spiritually strengthening. These words describe the best book you'll read this year. Dr. Saundra Dalton-Smith writes with honesty, wisdom, and practicality. *Being Fully Known* will inspire you, but it will also give you the tools to live your best life."

Carol Kent, founder and executive director of Speak Up Ministries, speaker, and author of *When I Lay My Isaac Down*

"I'm so excited about Dr. Saundra's new book *Being Fully Known*. She addresses critically important topics with wisdom and care for all of us to learn from and journey through as we deepen in living from our true identity in Christ. I know you will be impacted for the good!"

Stasi Eldredge, bestselling author of *Becoming Myself* and coauthor of *Captivating*.

"Dr. Saundra gives us more than a book—she gives us part of herself. Wisdom hard won and Biblical insight deeply mined are woven together in a love letter in a way that will change you in ways you never knew you needed. Highly recommended."

Margaret Feinberg, author of *The God You Need to Know*

"In *Being Fully Known*, our friend Dr. Saundra Dalton-Smith gives a biblical road map to understand how you can experience everything our Lord has for you. Her medical background, personal journey, and biblical insight lead you to become what your heart desires to be."

Phil and Debbie Waldrep, founders of Women of Joy

"In all our lives, there are moments when we wrestle with what feels like lost identity. With profound wisdom and authenticity, Dr. Saundra leads you to a place of belonging. This book is a treasure and belongs on the shelf of every person longing for soul transformation. When you're yearning to become all God intended you to be, this is your book! I can't recommend it highly enough! Bravo, Dr. Saundra!"

Becky Harling, conference speaker, John Maxwell certified leadership coach, and author of *Cultivating Deeper Connections in A Lonely World.*

"In *Being Fully Known*, beloved Women of Joy speaker and bestselling author Dr. Saundra Dalton-Smith beautifully expounds on the three key concepts of beholding, belonging, and becoming by understanding the truth of identity in Christ. Through personal illustrations from her twenty years as a general practice physician, Dr. Saundra sheds light on what happens when you surrender to God's timing. You no longer have to entertain condemnation, unworthiness, or shame. Come out of the shadows, exchange hiding from God and your past mistakes for being fully known. This book is for those who want accessible steps to move from burnout to breakthrough. Don't read this book unless you are seeking practical wisdom with insights on how to mature in Christ."

Sheryl Giesbrecht Turner, DTh., speaker and founder of From Ashes to Beauty, Inc. and The Widow Project, author of five books including *Unraveling the Lie-Knot*

"Our deep longing to be seen and known is incredibly complex. Dr. Saundra Dalton-Smith's words have a rhythm of a holy dance that deeply impact every part of our soul to unleash unlimited potential. As a medical doctor, Saundra understands the dynamics of human nature, and the added dimension of being a wise woman of God gives her deep spiritual insight. She is beautifully authentic and sometimes funny but always guides the reader to see possibilities beyond what they dream or imagine. I don't say this lightly when I tell you this book will change your life."

Heidi McLaughlin, award-winning
author and international speaker,
Heart Connection Ministry

"Saundra wrote this book for me. I wept my way through it, so personal was its message to my overachiever mindset and competitive character traits. There are phrases nestled among the pages of this book that I will remember as long as I live. The overarching message of 'beholding, becoming and belonging' will resonate in every person's heart. However, I believe this message will be especially powerful for women who have been victimized by the 'have it all, do it all, earn it all' mentality that has prevailed in the past fifty years. *Being Fully Known* invited me into an entirely different lifestyle. I am willing to be still and to joyfully know Him. Are you?"

Carol McLeod, blogger, Bible teacher,
podcaster, author of *Today is a Verb*

"Is it possible to embrace stillness over striving? *Being Fully Known* beckons weary travelers to find rest, not as an activity but as an awareness of a deep, abiding relationship with a loving God. Dr. Saundra fills every page with wisdom and wonder. *Being Fully Known* is not only an invitation to slow down and savor the goodness of God, it is a sanctuary."

Angela Donadio, author, ministry leader, and
founder of Communicators' Collective

DR. SAUNDRA DALTON-SMITH

BEING FULLY KNOWN

THE JOYFUL SATISFACTION OF BEHOLDING, BECOMING, AND BELONGING

estherpress

Books for Courageous Women
from David C Cook

BEING FULLY KNOWN
Published by Esther Press,
an imprint of David C Cook
4050 Lee Vance Drive
Colorado Springs, CO 80918 U.S.A.

Integrity Music Limited, a Division of David C Cook
Brighton, East Sussex BN1 2RE, England

Library of Congress Control Number 2024946886
ISBN 978-0-8307-8774-6
eISBN 978-0-8307-8775-3

The Team: Susan McPherson, Suzanne Gosselin, Gina
Pottenger, Dana Carrington, Susan Murdock
Cover Design: Gretchen Hyer

Printed in the United States of America
First Edition 2025

1 2 3 4 5 6 7 8 9 10

120624

CONTENTS

Part III: Belonging

You can access five bonus teaching videos by visiting
www.davidccook.org/access or scanning the QR
code with your phone. Use access code: known.

HOW TO USE
THIS BOOK

Dear Reader,

I am so delighted you've picked up *Being Fully Known*. Before you get started, let me provide a brief overview of what you will find inside. Being fully known is a journey of God-awareness, self-acceptance, and the fulfillment found in knowing you are seen and understood.

Throughout this book, you'll encounter a promise of deeper connection with God, feeling more fully yourself, and flourishing in the activities of your life. You'll be able to stop holding back and instead reveal who you really are—known, talented, and needed.

Within these pages you will discover how to:

- Welcome all parts of yourself.
- Access more goodness in your life.
- Live into what God sees in you.

- Connect with courage and authenticity.
- Embrace the fullness of your identity.

The book is divided into three main sections: Beholding, Becoming, and Belonging. Each chapter concludes with Scripture exploration and a Daily Unveiling section for personal reflection. Plus, I have included five bonus teaching videos you can access via the URL or QR code below. Don't run through these explorations. Take a leisurely walk. I recommend reading *Being Fully Known* with a friend or two and discussing your experiences over a twenty-one-day period. Check out the fasting guide at the end of the book for even more options. Allow ample time to experience the joyful satisfaction of beholding, becoming, and belonging. You are worth being fully known.

~ Dr. Saundra

Visit www.davidccook.org/access or scan this
QR code with the camera on your phone to
access the videos that accompany this book.

Access code: known

Chapter 1

THE UNKNOWN

Stillness. I can hear the water heating up in the coffeepot. The air purifier is humming in the next room, and my dog, Rosey, huffs at my feet. This isn't exactly stillness, but it will have to do.

My life is not still. There is usually something heating up, humming, or huffing. Is it possible to be still? Can the mind cease rehearsing? Can the will stop striving? Can the soul surrender to rest?

I try again. *Be still. Breathe. Stop. Relax. Sigh.* Life keeps moving. Try as I may, I can't manufacture stillness.

Years ago, achieving stillness might have been easier. Phones were attached to walls, not buzzing in your pocket. Work was confined to a specific location where you clocked in and out and rarely brought it home. Information had to be sought out in a *quiet* library, thumbing through a card catalog. Now you can have dozens of browser windows open at once, providing detailed information on any topic you desire. As a society, we excel at staying busy, taking on more and more. We have mastered the doing, but it has taken a toll. The constant doing has left us exhausted, overwhelmed, and heavyhearted as we process the onslaught of negative news. We produce much, but sometimes with little satisfaction.

When your striving only leaves you feeling emptier, you've stepped into dangerous, soul-sickening territory. Money does not bring you happiness. Laughter does not come naturally. Peace is elusive. Joy has fled. When I found myself in this place of unrest, God met me there. I was burned out in every area of my personal and professional life. I was in uncharted territory with a soul-deep fatigue that carved me out and opened room for God to move. The only frequency I could tune into was rest. I craved it above all else.

One day, I found myself flat on my back on my foyer floor. I hadn't fallen. It was the first time I'd intentionally paused to reflect on the direction of my life. My time on the cold hardwood was needed therapy. I realized that though there was ample activity in my days, my pursuits were not leading me to a place of joy or satisfaction. I needed a deeper level of rest that could help me recover my life, renew my energy, and restore my sanity. When I finally stood from the floor, I was on a mission to uncover the science and biblical meaning of rest. That quest ultimately resulted in my book *Sacred Rest*.

I spent over ten years of my life learning how to rest well. I grew my knowledge in the field until I was invited to share on stages around the world about the practicality, principles, and biblical precepts of rest. I am blessed to know that thousands of people have broken free from burnout using my 7 Types of Rest Framework™ and online assessment at RestQuiz.com. I am awed by the doors God has opened. I love the work He has allowed me to do, training leaders within churches, non-profits, and corporations to honor His command to rest. I am equally troubled by the missing pieces—the aspects of rest many struggle to embrace.

As I was signing books during one event, a young woman approached me and let out a long sigh. I didn't know if her prolonged exhale was a sign of relief or longing. She leaned over the high-top table and grabbed me by both forearms. Now, I'm a big-boned girl. I don't typically feel threatened in crowds. I've done enough kickboxing classes to believe I could uppercut my way out of most situations, but the force of this young woman's grip had me a little concerned. Before my panic alarms could go off, her first tear fell, hitting the cover of the book lying on the table between us. She wept with the desperation of a woman who had nothing to hide. Clinging to me, she cried, "I don't know how to stop *doing* when it all depends on me!"

The remaining women in the line took a collective step forward in response to her distress. The depth of the well of this woman's pain had force and pulled me in. Her statement held an honesty many could relate to in their own situations. Her words revealed a soul arrested by the truth of discontentment amid endless activity. My heart bent toward hers. I could have provided kind words, but the lump in my throat blocked all sound. Mute in the presence of a divine moment. Her eyes locked on a spot on the ground. She released her grasp on my arms abruptly and apologized. "I am so sorry. I don't know what came over me."

Emotional layers are a protective mechanism. They develop throughout our lives, helping us navigate the various feelings we encounter through our experiences. Outward layers can appear one way—confident, funny, stoic, reserved—while deep within, more vulnerable feelings are hidden from view. I watched as the woman's emotional layers moved back into their assigned places. Self-protection, inauthenticity, and fearfulness arose. A wall was erected before me. Tears retreated. Composure came. The only evidence of the outpouring I had just witnessed were the tears merging with the waters pictured on the cover of *Sacred Rest*. She was ready to drop it and move on. I was not. It's hard to move on from a place where God is actively moving. We chatted for a few moments as I went through the formalities of signing her book. I have no idea what I wrote on those pages. My thoughts were swirling as she shared more of her story.

"Be still, and know that I am God." This verse, Psalm 46:10, was the source of her lament. It's a seemingly impossible holy invitation. On the surface, it sounds like an invitation to rest. Underneath flows a depth that rivals the ocean. It's the DNA of a deeper relationship. When we let it replicate, it permeates everything. It's a call to fully understand who God is and who we become because of Him.

This calm isn't external but internal. Stillness is a "settledness" of the soul where questions lie down in the green pastures of trust and fears drown in the waters of love. It's where striving ceases, and the doing is done. You can simply be. This is the *being* of rest—the deeper work of resting well. Self-care and self-improvement will only get you so far. Stillness is the part that remains. Failure to understand both the being (still) and the knowing (He is God) will only achieve partial rest.

My lack of understanding is the part God is still revealing to me. I was raised to try hard at everything I did. For decades, I found comfort in the doing and the doing it well. I acclimated to a world where approval is attached to my performance and worth is allocated in direct response to what I do. When there is no action, I feel unvaluable and left behind. I judge myself as failing at work and at home. I trade stillness for busyness and being known for convenience. In resting, I found ways to recover from the busyness. I discovered strategies for making the inconvenience of restorative practices tolerable. Yet the need to be and be known remains. There is still more I need to learn. The need to be free from the fear of what others think when they see me being free, open, vulnerable, and transparent. The need to be delivered from confusion and complacency. The need to be awakened to boldness and arise in confidence. The need to know my worth independent of my work. The need to be baptized in His love, bathed in His Word, and led by His wisdom.

These lessons result from the transformational work of physical, mental, spiritual, emotional, social, sensory, and creative rest. Through these forms of rest, the unknown is made known. A part of experiencing these concepts requires God to do inside of you what He can only accomplish when you choose to be still and know He is God. It is the rest of beholding God in all things, becoming like Jesus, and living from a place of belonging. No longer wondering if God is for you but realizing He is always with you. No longer trying to become someone but being who you already are. No longer searching for the places where you fit in but resting in the places where you fit.

Let It Be

Being and doing represent two distinct parallels of existence and engagement with the world. Each offers its own unique depth and significance. Each has value. *Being* invites you to embrace the present

moment. It welcomes times of mindfulness and self-reflection, allowing you to savor the beauty of life's experiences without the pressure
of external expectations. Being makes room to see God at work in
the splendor of everyday circumstances. Conversely, doing involves
activity. It opens space for God to move through you, inviting you into
contribution. *Doing* is the manifestation of gifts and the expression of
talents.

Striking a balance between being and doing is as impossible as
finding a work-life balance. Balance neither exists, nor, I would come to
realize, is it what I really desire. I don't want my doing and being on different sides of the pendulum. I prefer they exist in harmony with each
other, where being and doing fellowship around the cross, enabling me
to honor both my need for inner satisfaction and my desire to impact
the world for Christ. Joyful satisfaction arises when we blend these
two aspects of existence. And we can cultivate a sense of wholeness in
our lives as we learn three key areas of being—beholding, becoming,
and belonging.

The word *behold* appears over a thousand times in literal transla-
tions of the Bible, in both the Old and New Testaments. It is used to
draw attention to something important to see, gaze upon, perceive, or
contemplate. Behold is an invitation to witness something you would
otherwise miss without it being pointed out to you. It's a call to be still
and take notice. Where Psalm 46:10 says, "Be still," I think it's helpful to consider the idea of beholding: *Behold* (look upon, reflect, take
notice) "and know that I am God."

What do you behold? Between my social media feeds, the laptop,
and the TV, there isn't much room left for beholding. It's easier to fill

my time with scrolling, searching, and watching than it is to look at how God is showing up in my life. Beholding points me back to God to receive insights into His character, witness His mighty works, and meditate on truth I have not ingested. Beholding illuminates His perspective. It elevates my ability to trust and rest, as beholding is the bridge between the two. I can only rest at the level of my trust in God. In beholding, I see God in multiple dimensions—alpha and omega, author and finisher, lion and lamb. By beholding God, I become aware of Him beholding me. And through this process, I begin to become what I behold.

Every day you are becoming. It is an outward expression of the inner work of what you behold. You are shaped by what has touched your life, your heart, your emotions, your motives, your aspirations, and your relationships. Becoming reflects what has captured your gaze. If your day-to-day is lacking satisfaction, you may have sacrificed *becoming* on the altar of routine, busyness, and comfort. Becoming is gloriously unpredictable. There are no schedules, time lines, or guidebooks. It has no map, and the only compass available is the Holy Spirit. You can't reason your way through because it's not a destination. It's a way of being where you are willing to be mentored from above.

Beholding points me back to God to
receive insights into His character,
witness His mighty works, and meditate
on truth I have not ingested.

Beholding and becoming naturally lead you into belonging. Belonging quiets all lesser forms of acceptance. When the performing ends and you stop attempting to please others, joy bursts through the clouds. The darkness lifts, and with it, the reliance on your own abilities, your own strength, and your own independence. You can see where you have been graced and favored by God intentionally and strategically. The pieces of your life come into alignment with your circumstances to usher in the full realization that Christ in you is enough.

Unfortunately, at the time the young woman at my book table grabbed hold of me, I was so early in my own processing of Psalm 46:10 that I had little hope to offer her. Though it was years after I had written *Sacred Rest*, stillness remained elusive. I understood her struggle to put being still into practice because it was also my struggle. I knew how to rest but not how to be still. Stillness was the unknown missing part of my understanding.

There were many moments of refreshing and times of restoration, but life remained a whirlwind in motion. There was no solace for the relentless demands and ceaseless distractions that warred against the stillness prescribed by the verse. Yet, the Word of God promises there is still sanctuary amidst the chaos—a sacred space where we can retreat to behold, become, and belong. It's a reminder to turn away from the noise and bright lights and to put our attention on God. This stillness is not focused on the absence of movement but rather on who is moving. It highlights with steadfast assurance that God is at work while we rest.

We can't be still because we don't know who God is, who we are, and where we fit. Living out the wisdom of Psalm 46:10 isn't merely about finding fleeting moments of respite. It's an ongoing practice of being over doing, where we can listen deeply to the whispers of our souls and attune ourselves to the gentle rhythms of grace. The fullness of joy is found in beholding God's power in the ordinary, becoming like Christ, and knowing you belong. True fulfillment arises not from our external achievements but from becoming what and who we behold—a gracious, compassionate Jesus whose yoke is light. God has made us for Himself, and we can never know rest and satisfaction until we know Him.

In the following pages, I reveal what I would now say to this young woman and others who:

- Find stillness impossible to practice.
- Lack confidence in their ability to wholly follow God.
- Value working and doing over resting and being.
- Question why their talents and gifts do not align with their current career and life.
- Jump from idea to idea but rarely stay with one to completion.
- Wrestle with confusion over the next right steps.
- Feel oppressed by the weight of past pain and trauma.
- Allow their voices to be silenced by fear but have much to say.
- Shrink back when placed in unfamiliar situations.
- Give God their yes but are hesitant to move at His pace.

The Beholding, Becoming, and Belonging sections of this book address each of these problems and more. There is a type of rest that yet remains. This is the rest of being fully known. It breaks down our walls of self-preservation and leaves us prostrate before the Lord. It bows our life to the one true God. Today is your opportunity to decide if you are willing to be still and know Him. To see His faithfulness in the mundane. To stand in awe of His grace transforming your greatest hurts, needs, and desires. To savor the experience of being welcomed and wanted. A life of joyful satisfaction is available to you!

Daily Unveiling

"But we all, with unveiled face, beholding as in a mirror the glory of the Lord, are being transformed into the same image from glory to glory, just as by the Spirit of the Lord."

—2 Corinthians 3:18 (NKJV)

Each chapter concludes with opportunities for you to intentionally practice uncovering truth and discovering new aspects of who God is and who you are. These are thoughts to sit with as you go about your daily life to experience the gentle work of being over doing. I pray these moments of God-awareness, reflection, and self-discovery elevate your faith, break through mindset barriers, and spark curiosity.

1. Your layers serve a purpose, or they would not exist. What are the benefits of your emotional layers?

2. God sees beyond the layers to the heart of the matter. Ask Him to reveal to you what He sees.

3. Each layer is an opportunity to know God and yourself at a deeper level. How deep are you willing to go? Pray this simple prayer: "God, show me more of you today."

Chapter 2

UNSEEN POSSIBILITY

"You haven't changed in years."

This is a phrase I hear often. I hear it from high school friends after they view my latest selfie on social media. I hear it from relatives whom I only see during holidays. I hear it from old associates I run into after many years. I don't know whether to take the statement as a compliment or an insult.

I suppose I understand why they would say this. I've kept the same hairstyle for the past twenty years. That's who I am. I resist change. I prefer consistency. I like predictability. I like to know as much as I can know. I like to control as much as I can control, because then I feel safe and protected. Maybe you know that feeling too. You hang out in comfortable crowds. You say yes to opportunities that fit into your scope of experience—activities you've done in the past. You move forward with undertakings you feel reasonably confident you can be successful doing. This is the reason I laugh out loud when I look at my current life. It feels completely out of my control ... which also feels like living.

I spend many weeks out of the year traveling for speaking engagements. I love experiencing different areas and cultures. I am always honored to be invited, but my favorite part isn't enjoying the location or even speaking from the stage; my favorite part is what happens after. I love that moment when a man or a woman comes up to me to share their story. I call it an "I see you moment." This is a moment when we stand eye to eye looking past each other's walls and see beyond the superficial.

I experienced one such "I see you moment" many years ago on Mother's Day. A church had invited me to speak during their Sunday morning service. Mother's Day had always been a day I dreaded. It was a tangible reminder of all I had missed growing up without a mother. I shared about that experience from the stage and how God had redeemed it by helping me to trust Him with the disappointments I had suffered. After the closing prayer, a woman came up to me and wrapped her arms around me in one of the most loving embraces I have ever experienced. She saw me. She understood that even when God redeems, the pain of loss can remain. She understood that, sometimes, the only sufficient words of comfort are unspoken.

Can you spot the "I see you moments" in your life?

Maybe you've been too busy filling your day with external things to notice them. What fillers do you prefer? Mine have always come wrapped in milk chocolate. Have you tried the fudge-covered Oreos? They should come with a warning: "Girl, say goodbye to whatever size pants you've been wearing and invest in elastic." Perhaps you prefer other fillers like shopping or sex or wine or TV. Where do you run when you feel empty? Who do you become when you feel unseen, unappreciated, unloved, and unworthy? Resist the pull toward shame. How you answer that question isn't a mirror of who you are. It is only a reflection of the survival skills you've picked up along the way. What's picked up can be released. You can always choose something new.

Start by seeking the "I see you moments" in your life. Look for the opportunities to open the door and let another person in. Take advantage of the openings to risk transparency and kindness, or to share love and encouragement. Look for moments to be the most unreserved version of yourself, to live in freedom and authenticity that attracts others to you.

For me, when the mic is silenced and the spotlights dim, that's when truth rides in. I always try to leave time after my speaking events for those "I see you moments." Having a conversation with someone across the book table and hearing her share how the talk resonated with her or how she recognizes herself in my story are the moments that stick with me. During one season of my life, I would intentionally look the person in the eye and say, "I see you." That's when I learned how much we instinctually fight being seen. I didn't expect pushback to my overtures of love and acceptance, but those simple words exposed a war inside people's souls.

I've watched the eyes of the biggest and toughest men glisten with tears or glance away in shame. I've witnessed women dissolve into sobs in my arms or strike back, like a viper, with venomous words. Both reactions surprised me. Who knew the words "I see you" would cut to the heart? I think the strong reactions to those words reveal the human fear of being fully known. It hearkens back to when Adam and Eve hid in the garden after eating the forbidden fruit. They created clothes for themselves so they would not feel so exposed. I have battled the tug-of-war between allowing others to know the real me and pretending to be who I think they desire.

At my speaking engagements, when I said, "I see you," they heard, "I see the parts of you you've been hiding. I see the abilities and dreams you've shut down. I see the gifts you've neglected and the places where experiences and people have left you feeling 'not enough.' I see the times when hope rose only to be shut down by disappointment. I see those days when you tried; you finally gathered up the courage and stepped out, only to fail. Courage is like wind and can be momentary. What you needed was the sustaining power of energy, purpose, conviction, and intentionality."

I see you.

I see you sitting there thinking about what could be, and what would have been "if only..." If only you took a chance, if only you stepped out, if only you got past your fears. I see you weighing the available possibilities against the barriers on the scales of time. I see you slaying the Goliath of negative self-chatter and finally seeing yourself through the lens of what could be.

What if the "more" you're looking for isn't more stuff you can pay for with your credit card or acquire through a higher paying job or more business contracts? What if it's not more friends or more social media followers or more attention and love from others? What if it's not a better body or a cleaner house or perfect children?

What if the more you're looking for is not external but internal?

Could it be that the more you seek is more of you? More of you showing up every day in your life confident, assured, passionate, purposeful, and engaged. More of you at peace with yourself. At peace with the way you laugh too loud and occasionally snort if the joke hits hard. At peace with the freckles on your face or the mole on your chin. At peace with the extra jiggle in your thighs and spreading of your hips. What if the more you're looking for is more of who God designed you to be?

Could it be this more you seek requires not settling? Not giving in with a sense of defeat or indifference. Not denying there are places for improvement and growth, but at peace with who you are *now*, at this exact moment, so that you can be present and enjoy today. This more involves not looking toward the future and focusing only on the pleasure to come, nor holding onto a past that keeps you cemented in what you cannot change, but instead embracing the present, experiencing the many beautiful facets of your life.

The more begins with you. It begins with recognizing what you have been saying yes to and what your yeses are costing you. There have been seasons of my life where I only said yes to the easy and comfortable. I gave my yeses to things that didn't stretch me or, at times, even move me. I spent my yeses like Monopoly money, throwing them around like I was at a bargain sale. I snatched up things quickly without evaluating if they fit or would become one more thing hanging in the closet of my life taking up space.

Some of my yeses have been costly like the yes given when asked if I would help with the bake sale at my son's school. As someone who has little aptitude for cooking, this should have been an automatic no. I knew whipping up baked goods was not my talent, but mom guilt is real. I reasoned my "yes" to this would make up for the times when work caused me to miss soccer games and school plays. Unfortunately, the wrong "yes" became a self-inflicted punishment that ended up costing me time, energy, and a large catering bill at the local bakery!

How many yeses are you giving to things that don't move your heart to compassion or move your soul to hunger for greater things? What tasks are you doing that don't move your mind to creativity and innovation? What yeses are preventing you from moving your hands to joyful action? Most of us say yes to a lot of things—pursuits that fill our plates and overwhelm our calendars. At times, these obligations leave us utterly exhausted to the point of despair. Our yeses must be for *more*. Our yeses need to be for those things that stretch us beyond our self-imposed limitations, allowing us to break free into the *more* we already possess inside. This stretching is not tiresome; it welcomes the breaking of the dawn to experience a fuller life and existence.

Never Say Never

For my fiftieth birthday, the gift I chose to give myself was the gift of conquering one of my I-could-nevers. I decided to run my first marathon. My husband, Bobby, is an ultramarathon runner and Ironman athlete. He's the type of person who is disciplined, dedicated, and intentional in his actions. If he says he's going to do a thing, it's as good as done. It matters little what obstacles get in the way, the difficulty of the situation, or how impossible it may seem. When he says something, he means it. He is a man of his word.

For the past ten years, I've stood on the sidelines watching him run his races and participate in great feats of athleticism. At a marathon, the few hours of waiting pass quickly. But the Ironman races can take up to eleven hours. I get up early to cheer him on at the starting line, and I am there waiting at the finish line when he runs in. Bobby has even run a one-hundred-mile ultramarathon! Now that truly is an all-day and -night event, from sunrise to sunrise. He actually finished it in just under twenty-four hours, allowing us to leave right before the first ray of light broke over the horizon of Alabama's beautiful Lake Martin.

I've always been proud of my husband's accomplishments and enjoyed being his biggest cheerleader. Watching him train is therapeutic for my soul. Bearing witness to the hours of dedication he pours into the process is humbling and inspiring! His blistered feet and achy back, the muscle fatigue and sore joints that get pounded and strained during the training—all these physical realities testify that the choice to persevere comes with a cost. There can be no finishing without the price of perseverance.

I have watched it all. I've seen the discomfort of the process and joy of a dream fulfilled when the training and preparation pay off. I've sat on the sidelines encouraging him as he goes through each checkpoint, sending texts of encouragement to his watch: "You got this!" or "Keep going, you're almost there!" I was excited to be a part of his journey and celebrate his accomplishments, all while thinking, *I could never.*

Physically, I am healthy. My I-could-never wasn't about what I thought my body could do but rather about who I believed I was. I could never be as disciplined as my husband. I could never push my body that hard. I could never accomplish a goal with such a high cost of time and physical effort.

Eight months before my March birthday, I began to train. I signed up to run a local marathon during my birthday month. I sensed my perseverance growing as I added mile upon mile to my long runs. The week before my marathon, my son broke his ankle, and he had surgery two days before my race. On the day of my marathon, I was distracted. As I ran, I would slow down or stop to text my family and make sure my son was getting his pain meds. Finally, he texted me: "My pain is doing better now. Run your race, Mom. Love you."

His words carried a deeper meaning for me. For years I had supported others as they ran their races. Now it was time for me to run *my* race, and the people who loved me most wanted me to run it. I didn't get the time I expected (because of all the text messaging), but I finished the race and discovered that I *could* run 26.2 miles.

What are your I-could-nevers? Where in your life do you find yourself sitting on the sidelines, observing, waiting, wishing? What are the occasions where you cheer others on while believing you could never succeed the way they do?

There are times when it's good to be on the sidelines. We should be there for our family members and friends, cheering them on when they're doing great things. I should be there for my husband when he's running an ultramarathon or my son when he's dribbling down the basketball court to shoot a game-winning basket at the buzzer. Celebrating others is one of the great joys of life. We should be on the sidelines when they're doing great things—not only when they're succeeding, but when we see them taking risks and stepping outside their comfort zones. We should be on the sidelines cheering for them, encouraging them, and pushing them to finish strong.

Sideline moments are opportunities to take a break, celebrate others, and pour out your love and support. Sideline moments keep us in a place of humility where jealousy and envy are banished. On the sidelines, we sacrifice our needs, wants, and desires, so we can appreciate the needs, wants, and desires of others. Those sideline moments keep us human. But to really live, to truly share *you*—your gifts and talents—there are times when you must get off the sidelines and into the game.

Maybe your sideline has looked like years spent mothering, where you've put your own needs and desires on hold so you can coach and care for others. Perhaps your sideline looks like staying in a career or position you no longer find rewarding. The role may have been a good fit for a season, the place you were supposed to be for a time, but seasons end, and times change. If you stay within a season that has concluded, you're on the sideline. Or maybe you've let others take center stage, holding back or hiding the abilities and talents you possess.

For some it's been so long since you've felt like an active participant, you don't even realize you're on the sidelines. Being sidelined has become a way of life. Those on the sidelines are usually alert and paying attention. They're ready to jump up to cheer or jump in and play at any moment. They stand in anticipation of an opportunity. They desire to engage and have a hunger to participate. They are ready to step into the action.

Maybe you're not even on the sidelines anymore; you're all the way up in the stands. You've slipped into your most comfy clothes and grabbed your popcorn, Skittles, and diet soda. You're ready to be enthusiastic for everybody except yourself. I'm not judging you. I can relate. I know this feeling well because I've lived it. I've looked on jealously from the stands at women who dared to live freely. I've hungered to be one who could show up without the shackles of people-pleasing. I've secretly berated myself for lacking the confidence to move from the stands to the locker room and change my garments. The shift requires me to make a decision: I can sit comfortably in the stands, or I can choose to step into the game and engage with all that is available to me.

Standing Ovation

While we sit in the stands, we have a lot of time. Right about now your thoughts may be yelling, *My life is packed! I'm super busy! I have no time!* It's a lie. We all get the same twenty-four hours each day—the one living, the one waiting, and the one watching. What makes the difference is what we say yes to and the experiences those yeses bring our way.

There can be joy in the waiting. We may find peace in the watching and derive a sense of purpose from supporting those in the game. Time is not our enemy. Time does not dictate whether you are in the stands, on the sidelines, or in the game. How we choose to show up in our lives comes from a place deeper than the numbers on a clock or the dates on a calendar. There is a season for everything, including time on the sidelines. But when we remain in that seat past its appointed season, we create discontentment as we chronically diminish our own needs and desires for the benefit of others. When we realize we have relegated ourselves to the sidelines, we may experience inner turmoil because it demands us to answer hard questions, such as:

1. Who am I apart from my relationships (marriage, parenting status, singleness, etc.)?

2. How can I still be me as I change physically (aging, weight, disability)?

3. What value do I offer others when I'm simply being and not always doing?

4. Who am I apart from my roles (job, titles, degrees)?

5. How will I change after this life transition (wedding /divorce, new parenthood/empty-nest, job loss/ promotion, death of a loved one, etc.)?

We label these seasons with terms like quarterlife or midlife crisis. But I believe "crisis" is the wrong word. The discomfort of life transitions and discovering who you really are apart from titles, relationship status, and physical appearance is healing. You are healing from the imbalance of doing and being within your soul. The loss of attachments and descriptors that no longer serve you, the things that have held you back from living fully, can be painful and feel disorienting and chaotic. But as you press in, you will discover greater purpose on the other side.

As we prepare to move into the three parts of this book, I want to lay a foundation on which we can stand in these first three chapters. I will not be providing a step-by-step approach or structured framework for you to follow. The foundation I'm providing is an uncommon one. It has no structure, but it is stabilizing. It has no weight, but it is weighty. It has no walls because it goes beyond all limitations. It is the foundation God shared with Moses in Exodus 3:14 when Moses asked His name. The answer, "I AM," is the foundation of the transformation coming into your life. God's Spirit inside of us. Infinite possibility wrapped in flesh. The Unseen at work within what is seen. God visible through you.

If you could see the great cloud of witnesses mentioned in Hebrews 12, you would be overcome by the multitude of people in eternity cheering you on. They are on the sidelines because they have finished their race and gone before you. There is a standing ovation celebrating every time God is visible through your being and doing. They cheer as you lay down your limiting beliefs, your pride, and your misaligned priorities. They clap as you relinquish the places where your voice is tolerated in search of places where it is celebrated—places where your smile is real, your laugh flows freely beside your tears, and all of you is welcomed.

The place where you can truly be yourself does exist. It's both inside of you and outside of you. I have discovered that it is almost impossible to find the external places you fit until you feel settled with who God has created you to be—both strengths and weaknesses. And you can't fully appreciate that design apart from knowing God's Spirit. So this is where we will begin, searching for what's within you. We will chip away at the voices that have tried to shut you up and keep you sidelined by replacing them with the Voice of Truth. We will cut away the guilt and the shame attached to your time in the bleachers and peel away the years that seem wasted to reveal how they have equipped you for deeper intimacy with God and others. Finally, we will seek to redeem past experiences, both helpful and unhelpful, uncovering the ways they have prepared you for the places where you fit today!

I thank God for passing time and changing seasons. Let these reminders of nature be the catalyst to kindle your soul, igniting the dry wood of *hope* that remains inside you. May it start a fire in your belly that allows you to stand and shout to the parts of you that have yet to be invited to living fully.

Whether you are thirty, fifty, or seventy-five matters not. This process of becoming all circles back to the more you seek. So, let me ask again for the people seated in the last row of the bleachers: What if the more you are seeking is not outside of you but inside of you, lovingly deposited there by the Great I AM?

As you see God's Spirit within you, you will be amazed at who you can become. Let Him surprise you with *more of you*—bold, confident, loving, free, joyful, courageous, committed, powerful, peaceful, authentic, giving, trusting, connected. The possibilities are endless.

Daily Unveiling

1. Where do you currently see yourself: watching, waiting, or living?

2. Think about an activity you enjoy watching or a person you greatly admire. What characteristics are you celebrating as you watch him or her living fully?

3. You are worthy of celebration. Can you see yourself as valued and cherished? Pray this simple prayer: "God, open my eyes to see myself clearly."

Chapter 3

UNSPOKEN TRUTHS

The home was nestled along a flawless strand of beach on a slight rise that overlooked the gently curving coastline. A fusion of modern architecture and natural beauty, the structure boasted a view where white sand met turquoise waters. Each room featured a nautical theme, and every square inch welcomed me in. From the front foyer to the sprawling backyard on display from the cozy screened-in porch, I was in love! I was carried away by the whimsical beach house ... being featured on HGTV. It was my dream home and one my logic told me would never be within my reach.

How do you view what's possible? Many of us base what we can accomplish on past experiences or what our parents or grandparents achieved. Some of us set goals based on what we have seen others achieve. Maybe your definition of the possible stems from what you believe you can control or bring about by your own strength. Sometimes what we judge as *impossible* is, more accurately, *improbable*. It is possible for you to win the HGTV dream home sweepstakes, but it's highly improbable.

Even a one-in-a-million chance creates a possibility. We often call things impossible when the truth is probability is low.

When we struggle to discern between what is impossible versus what is improbable, we create a barrier to getting off the sidelines and living. Things that feel impossible often just require significant effort or a change in our mindset. A key to seeing the difference is distinguishing between truth and perception. Philippians 4:8 tells us, "Finally, brothers and sisters, whatever is true, whatever is noble, whatever is right, whatever is pure, whatever is lovely, whatever is admirable—if anything is excellent or praiseworthy—think about such things." Your perception of what is true will be the North Star guiding every decision and directing your thoughts.

Picture yourself holding a rose, delighting in its rich fragrance, vibrant colors, prickly stem, and velvety petals. With a sense of certainty, you would declare these qualities as undeniable truths about the flower. But what if your friend, unbeknownst to either of you, lacked the sense of smell? In her experience, the rose has no fragrance. Two conflicting truths emerge—one is factually true, and the other is experientially true.

In this situation, you might attribute this difference of truth to your friend's inability to perceive scents. You would judge your experience as accurate and your friend's as missing important details. Now consider a scenario where nobody, not even you, could detect the rose's scent. In such a world, the truth of the rose's fragrance loses significance as it becomes buried beneath layers of inaccessible perception. Since no one can experience the aroma, we assume its existence must not be a factual truth. The question shifts. Instead of, "What is truth?" we ask, "To what shared experiences among individuals are we attributing truth?"

This intricate dance between truth and perspective can either draw us closer to God or become a stumbling block to beholding, becoming, and belonging. Here's an example: I worked as a medical doctor for twenty years, and I have never seen blind eyes opened, or a paralyzed person walk. During medical school, I spent months in gross anatomy class, and never once did a corpse arise from the table. To me, these supernatural occurrences seem like impossibilities, but is it more accurate to say they are improbabilities? What is true? My lack of experience with the supernatural does not make it less true that such events have occurred. The numbness of my senses does not diminish the power of God.

We must recognize that our personal truths are intricately woven into the fabric of our individual viewpoints. When our experiences vary, so do our perceptions of truth. Truth is independent of our limited human knowledge. Truth stands firm, unaffected by our limited understanding. Truth is the bedrock of existence and the unwavering beacon that guides us through the complexities of life. It transcends our perceptions and exists beyond the confines of our subjective experiences. Truth is not merely a product of what we know or believe; it exists independently of our comprehension. When we are aware of this, we can approach truth with humility and an appreciation for what we have yet to experience.

Our quest for truth requires a humble
and contrite spirit, and a willingness to
recognize the limits of our own knowledge.

From the Scriptures we learn that the source of truth is God and His Word (John 17:17). His truth beckons us to seek clarity and wisdom; it urges us to transcend our preconceptions. Truth is not always easily discerned. It may be obscured by layers of our own erroneous beliefs. Our quest for truth requires a humble and contrite spirit, and a willingness to recognize the limits of our own knowledge. It demands introspection, daily unveiling, and a readiness to confront the unknown.

Truth is the cornerstone of wisdom and the rock on which we must build our understanding. It invites us to explore, question, and grow in discernment. Ultimately, embracing truth empowers us to navigate life with clarity, integrity, and purpose. When Jesus was on earth, He made a bold claim when He said, "I am the way and the truth and the life. No one comes to the Father except through me" (John 14:6).

My non-believing friends often question me about my faith in a two-thousand-year-old Savior. They may accept His historical existence; however, His life, miracles, and claim to be the "only way" to God is difficult for them to swallow. My response to their questions is always the same: "Once you experience Him, you will know He is the Truth." This is also my response to anyone who has put initial trust in Christ but has not experienced Him in other ways. You can know Him as Savior and yet have not taken hold of the "abundant life" He offers. Consider this list containing a few of the powerful names of Jesus found in Scripture. Put a check mark by the names of Jesus you have not yet experienced.

Bread of Life (John 6:35)
Chief Shepherd (1 Pet. 5:4)

Light of the World (John 8:12)

Prince of Peace (Isa. 9:6)

Redeemer (Job 19:25)

Rose of Sharon (Song 2:1)

Sun of Righteousness (Mal. 4:2)

The Door (John 10:9 NLV)

Lion of Judah (Rev. 5:5)

The truth of who Jesus is cannot be confined to our personal understanding of truth or stay within the limits of our experiences. This truth comes in like a tsunami and shatters the glass ceiling of our perception. Moving into a deeper experience with truth can take you into indescribable situations and powerful, undeniable encounters with God. As you overcome logic and probability with His truth, He will prove to you that the impossible is always possible with Him.

Belief

Imagine a belief as a pair of sunglasses. The lenses affect how you perceive the world around you and your view of what is possible. Likewise, your beliefs shape your thoughts and actions. But here's where things get interesting: your beliefs are not faithful or consistent. It's as if your sunglasses are shrinking the size of what you see in some situations and magnifying it in others. Problems can become giants with no solutions in sight and, conversely, we can dismiss things that should be a big deal. We hold tightly to our convictions, convinced what we see is an accurate picture and the only one to behold.

It's as if you're holding a treasure map, firmly believing it will lead you to a chest of gold. Upon closer examination, you realize the map might be outdated or inaccurate, but you choose to cling to the belief that it will guide you to the prize. Similarly, your erroneous beliefs and feelings can guide you down paths that don't align with the truth.

Let's delve into a common struggle many of us face: the belief that we are not good enough or that we do not measure up. This belief often creeps in through comparison, societal pressures, or a preoccupation with past failures. Though this belief is common, the truth we learn from Scripture does not focus on our shortcomings. The truth God imparts is that each of us is born with inherent worth and value, regardless of our flaws and failures. The belief in our inadequacy, which often gets pounded in by the world, doesn't align with the truth of our inherent worth as creations of God. This disconnect invites negative thoughts and emotions that undermine our confidence and self-esteem. When you believe you don't measure up, you may spend years trapped in a cycle of self-doubt, unable to recognize your true worth.

But what if you dare to challenge this faulty belief? What if you choose to align your beliefs about yourself with God's truth about your worth? By acknowledging and embracing the truth that you are of great worth to Him (Luke 12:7), you can begin to break free from the chains of feelings of inadequacy. You can begin to cultivate a mindset rooted in self-acceptance and compassion that empowers you to live authentically and confidently from a place of belonging.

Truth is the ground you stand on, while belief is the glasses you wear to see where you are walking. We rely on truth to be consistent and unchanging—like the sun rising each morning and setting at the end of the day. Belief, however, is founded on ideas that may shift or be flawed. Looking through a pair of polarized sunglasses may make things look darker, but that doesn't mean it's nighttime. Understanding the relationship between truth and belief, or the things we believe to be true, positions us to be discerning and question beliefs about ourselves and the world that no longer serve us.

Seeking to uncover the truth about God found in His Word is like peering into the depths of the ocean. Undisclosed treasures lie in its depths that no human eye has seen. No person has exhausted its resources or been able to quantify its limits. Think about that for a moment. God's truth isn't confined by human limitations. Our journey with God in this life isn't just about knowing His truth intellectually; it's about letting that truth seep into the fabric of who we are and affect every aspect of our lives. God doesn't only invite us to swim in the waters of His truth, He invites us to drink the Living Water that changes us from the inside out.

So how do we successfully navigate this journey of being fully known? We must begin with humility—the willingness to acknowledge that our understanding is limited. We must approach God's Word with open hearts and minds, ready to receive His truth even when it challenges our assumptions. But let's be real here: discerning God's truth doesn't just happen. It requires effort and intentionality—a willingness to dig deep, wrestle with difficult questions, and allow His truth to reshape our perceptions. If we give into His gentle guidance, a beautiful transformation will take place during this time of truth-seeking. As we immerse ourselves in God's presence and ask Him to show us who He is, we begin to see life through a different lens. His truth clarifies, bringing things into focus and shaping our decisions.

Right now, take a moment to reflect. How do you view the place of God's truth in your life? Are you willing to let that truth permeate every fiber of your being and rewrite your perceptions? Are you open to the transformative power of His truth? As you ponder these questions, may you find yourself drawn closer to the heart of God, where truth reigns.

In the pages ahead, we will embark on a journey of God-discovery, spiritual reformation, and personal transformation. We will engage with three central concepts: beholding, becoming, and belonging. Through these sections, we will navigate the intricate interplay between truth and belief to guide you toward a profound alignment of the two. This process can be uncomfortable and even feel chaotic, but what awaits you on the other side is freedom, peace, and joy. It's time to be whole. Wholly aware of your worth. Wholly convinced of your value. Wholly confident in God's care for you.

In Part I: Beholding, we start by acknowledging and accepting the greatness of God. Acceptance is the mental attitude that something is true and can be trusted. Within this section, we will explore God's love, power, grace, mercy, and authority. Beholding the fullness of God allows us to daily recognize His Spirit at work within us.

Next, in Part II: Becoming, we step into identity convergence, the concept of two or more things coming together to form a new whole. This is where we align our beliefs with the truth. Through guided introspection and reflection, you will bridge the gap between who you know yourself to be and who God is revealing you to be in Him. It's your opportunity to step into your strengths, gifts, and talents with confidence. Becoming isn't about self-actualization or striving for perfection; it's about embracing authenticity and finding peace in being yourself—the wonderful individual God created. You will leave this time with a clearer understanding of who you are and how the Holy Spirit is leading you.

Finally, in Part III: Belonging, we will emerge from the secret place of inner transformation and step out into view. As you embrace the transformative power of daily living aligned with God's truth and presence in your life, you will find renewed confidence in His ability to use you. It's about walking in the fullness of God. By integrating into your life the truths you've discovered, you will emerge empowered to live openly, honestly, and lovingly in the places where you fit. No longer hiding parts of your identity or trapped in a web of distorted beliefs and flawed perceptions, you will break through into the wide-open place of God's unlimited power and exciting plan for you.

Each chapter within these headings will include a challenging mindset shift. The purpose of each challenge is to shine a spotlight on your beliefs, causing you to evaluate if a belief is based on impossibility or improbability. Is the belief rooted in your perception or in God's immutable truth revealed in His Word? Together, the beholding, becoming, and belonging sections—along with their accompanying Daily Unveilings—will serve as a road map that aligns truth and belief, and guides you toward a deeper understanding of God, yourself, and the world around you.

With the focus in our world on human and artificial intelligence, many of us have forgotten how to be spirit-led. We overthink, research, and rationalize every decision. As we prepare to move into Part I: Beholding, I want to sound a clarion call to awaken your spirit to its rightful role in your life. May you experience a realignment where your spirit reclaims its place as the leader of your mind and body. Allow the hierarchy of your three-part being to be led by the Spirit of God within you, above your reasoning and understanding. Experience the greatness of God anew.

Daily Unveiling

1. Who or what has been leading your life journey—fears, desires, comfort, significant other, family, finances, God, etc.? (You may have multiple answers.)

2. Are there beliefs you hold that are holding you back? If these beliefs are not moving you closer to God, release your grasp on them.

3. Regardless of where you are on your journey, there is more of God to know and more of His truth to experience. Pray this simple prayer: "God, I want more of You."

Part I

BEHOLDING

Visit www.davidccook.org/access or scan
this QR code with the camera on your
phone to watch Beholding Video No. 2.

Access code: known

Chapter 4

UNEQUALED ADORATION

Yellow flowers in a clear crystal vase graced the nightstand. A loud metallic sound filled the room as I lowered the guardrails of the bed to listen to my patient's lungs. Stretched on the bed lay two bodies, my patient and his wife. Hospital beds are single occupancy. Typically, there is not enough room for company. But months of battling cancer had shrunk my patient's body down to half its prior size, leaving ample room. Days turned to weeks and weeks into a month in room 425. My daily visits varied from early mornings to late evenings and everything in between, depending on my call schedule. Each day she was by his side. Some days they would be sitting at the side of the bed talking or playing a board game. Other days they would be in the bathroom as she supported him through waves of nausea.

Lining the room were photographs brought to remind him of all there was to fight for. Wedding pictures and family photos revealed the smiling faces of people, I'm sure, who were supporting him.

During one of my visits, he was alone—a rare occasion when something had pulled his wife away from his bedside. "Where is your wife today?" I asked. "I'm not used to seeing you in here without her." His face grew pensive as he selected his words carefully. Twisting a straw in one hand while holding a protein shake in the other, he stared blankly into the distance and said, "I'm going to have to leave her."

I wasn't sure I had heard him correctly. My comment was intended to be small talk. In my attempt to be social, I had opened a conversation I wasn't anticipating. He continued, "We have been married for over forty years. How am I supposed to leave her?" There were no tears. Neither sadness nor fear would be correct definitions for his emotions. This looked like torture. His eyebrows arched, his forehead burrowed, and his lips pursed. His pain permeated the room. He looked up at me and declared, "I don't fear death. I know the Lord, and I've accepted Jesus as my Savior. I know where I'm going. I can deal with this cancer. What I can't deal with is watching her loving me, knowing I will soon be leaving her. Her pain is killing me."

The room door swung wide, and his wife walked in, holding up a bag. "I got your favorite tacos!" I watched as his lips turned up to share a weak smile with her. There was no chance to reply to his statement other than to give his shoulder a squeeze of acknowledgment as I left them alone. His words continued to linger in my thoughts: "I'm going to have to leave her." As if he had a choice in the matter. As if life had allowed him to make a reservation for his death date and he chose the early seating. The love expressed between the two of them warmed the space around them. It blanketed their interactions and held them. Every caress of the back, kiss on the cheek, and grasp of his hand held significance. One day those touches would be gone. Replaced by the memories of a great love.

Grounded in Love

That night I prayed for this couple. I asked God to give my patient peace during this end-of-life transition, and I lifted his wife in prayer. Opening my Bible, I landed on Lamentations 3:22–23, "The steadfast love of the LORD never ceases; his mercies never come to an end; they are new every morning; great is your faithfulness" (ESV).

Lord, no one loves like You, was the thought that came to my mind. Immediately, I heard the inner whisper of His still, small voice, "My love sits on both sides of the equation. It has no equal." An image of my patient and his wife filled my imagination. The hospital bed became a scale, and each sat on one side. The scale was balanced. Then one got up, but the scale did not move. It was as if it were broken, but I knew it was not. It did not move because the steadfast love of God sat on both sides of the scale alongside husband and wife.

It is hard to believe we can be loved with the depth of adoration God rains on us. His love is not shown primarily in blessings or favor or even in His goodness. The magnitude of His love is shown most in that He always remains near. Think about the times when you felt most deeply cherished. Long dinners staring into the eyes of your significant other, when no words were needed to communicate the emotions shared. Or the times you cherished others. Hours seated beside a parent, child, or friend in a hospital room lending your support. Outward expressions of steadfast love are seen in the ministry leader who continues to pour out, steadfast and faithful, regardless of the size of his or her audience. It's observed in mothers who arise early to intercede for a prodigal child or fathers who carry the burden of helping their family feel safe and protected. This is the weight of love.

When someone is near, they're close enough to see all your faults, frailties, insecurities, mistakes, and shortcomings. They can see past the outward facade. The unfiltered version of you is on display. When love is present, the heart declares, "I choose to know all of you and love you for all you are." Love is what keeps marriages faithful. It's the gravity that pulls you into proximity with people you cherish. It's the through line of the parent–child relationship and the reason a parent continues to pray and hope for a wayward child's return. Love remains. It does not change based on the other person's behavior. Like truth, love is a grounding force you can build on.

During my time volunteering with a nonprofit, we changed our location many times as the organization grew. At one potential site, there was much discussion about the property's location. We wanted to ensure the new office space would be easily accessible and inviting to the families we served. The building we were considering was old, forgotten, and abandoned. On the surface, it looked like an unworthy candidate. However, when the board members took a deeper look, we found the building to have a strong and stable foundation. Everything on the surface was easily restored with some plaster and paint. Now families throughout my city visit this building weekly to receive spiritual and tangible support. The accessibility and prominent location of the property is a constant reminder of the love available to those in need, and it began with someone looking beyond the exterior to see its foundational qualities.

Every person I know has had moments when they felt forgotten, overlooked, abandoned, or unworthy. No amount of positive self-talk can banish our quiet fear of being unlovable. We know ourselves too well. We have been present for every mistake. We have firsthand experience with each of our sins. We have witnessed ourselves breaking promises to others. We have broken promises to ourselves. We know our secret thoughts and hidden agendas. Our close affiliation with our flaws leads us to question whether we are worthy of love. We can't comprehend how anyone could love us as we are, and yet God does. He welcomes our exploration of His steadfast love. He rips the veil of separation between Himself and us, leaving it in a heap at His feet. He beckons us to come closer. He invites us into intimacy. He summons us to behold Him in all His glory.

Good Clay

During a spiritually and emotionally challenging period of my life when I was desperate for rest, I committed to putting in fifty hours of self-care during a three-month span. Logistically, it should have been doable, but my weekly calendar looked like a bingo card. Every square had an entry (or ten). Each hour, from the time I rose in the morning to the moment I smeared on my nightly under-eye cream, was jam-packed. There was little margin and certainly not room to squeeze in fifty hours of anything. But this wasn't just a frivolous desire or a good idea for me; it was a needed intervention. My life was cracked and could hold nothing good. There was no satisfaction. There was no joy. I had slipped back into work, work, and hey, how about a little more work.

So I took on the challenge with a do-or-die attitude. The previous few months I had been plagued by body aches, heart palpitations, and poor sleep—symptoms I experience when I'm stressed and approaching burnout. I committed to fitting in these needed fifty hours of nurturing myself. One of the self-care activities I decided on was a spinning class. Not the type of spinning class you'd find at the gym where twenty super-fit women huff and puff on bikes as they climb an imagined Mt. Everest. No, that is not how I recharge. This was a pottery spinning class at a local art store. If you are anywhere near my age, you probably just got the image of Patrick Swayze and Demi Moore sitting at the potter's wheel in the movie *Ghost*. I've always wanted to take one of these classes and was excited to find one within an hour's drive. I was even able to convince my husband to join me.

During this messy, playful class, I had a sobering revelation. I could not shake the feeling that I had little in common with the clay I was molding with my hands. It was pliable, supple, and yielding. It responded to even the slightest touch with graceful submission. It moved on the wheel without resistance. Good clay does not crack under the probing and the prodding of the potter's hands. It holds no opinion on what its finished form should be. It is content to be whatever the potter desires. But bad clay has attitude. Probe it for too long, and it will crack, leading to deformation and brokenness. There have been so many times when I've resisted the Potter's hands. In pride I've become misshapen and eventually full of cracks. Beholding the properties of good clay made me yearn for this type of relationship with the Potter.

Could this be the reason brokenness is allowed to be a part of our process? It is the quickest way to surrender. It overcomes our stubbornness and bypasses our resistance. Cracks in our clay open us up so the tears can flow to soften the hard places and make us more capable of yielding to the Potter's touch. Perhaps brokenness is not a flaw but rather an integral part of the process to grow in intimacy with the Potter. Could it be that, in my brokenness, I experience my truest surrender? Brokenness has a unique way of shattering stubbornness, dismantling pride, and paving the way for a deeper connection with God and others.

Where has brokenness entered your life? Perhaps you've experienced the wounding of illness, trauma, divorce, death, betrayal, failure, disappointment, or another area where pain lives. Every crack and fracture in my being serves as a canal through which God can flow, bypassing the barriers I erect around my heart and bringing healing. In those moments of vulnerability, when my defenses crumble, I become accepting of the Potter's touch. Like the clay on the wheel, I allow myself to be molded and shaped by the hands of God. Each imperfection becomes a testament to the beauty of surrender. Through brokenness, I am stripped of my illusions of control and forced to confront the truth of my humanity. It is in this raw, exposed state that I find the courage to yield to God's touch, allowing His transformative power to mold me into something of His choosing.

So perhaps being "bad clay" is not a flaw to be ashamed of but rather a necessary step in the journey toward true surrender and transformation. Embracing my brokenness allows me to relinquish my grip on self-reliance and open myself up to the healing touch of the Potter. It is through the cracks in my armor that the light of grace seeps in, illuminating the path toward wholeness and restoration. As I walk this journey of surrender, I am reminded that even in my brokenness, I am held, cherished, and endlessly loved by the One who formed me from the dust of the earth. In the surrendering, I decrease, and God increases. In my yielding, His greatness is in on display for the world to behold.

Here are a few Scriptures to ground you in the truth of beholding the love of God. Let His Word be the lens through which your beliefs are framed.

Behold the Love of God

1 John 3:1 — "See what great love the Father has lavished on us, that we should be called children of God! And that is what we are! The reason the world does not know us is that it did not know him."

Practical application — Behold the extravagant love the Father has poured out on you by calling you His child. Take time to reflect on the magnitude of this truth: you are not merely a servant or casual acquaintance but a beloved child of the Most High God. Allow the truth of being His child permeate every aspect of your life, shaping your identity and influencing your actions. Live each day with the confidence and assurance that you belong to God's family, and let this reality empower you to walk in love and show grace to others. As you embrace your identity as a beloved child of God, allow His love to shine through you, illuminating the darkness of the world and drawing others into the light of His love.

Isaiah 43:1 — "But now, thus says the LORD, who created you, O Jacob, and He who formed you, O Israel: 'Fear not, for I have redeemed you; I have called you by your name; you are Mine'" (NKJV).

Practical application — Take time to meditate on the truth that God has redeemed you and called you by name. Reflect on the significance of being claimed as God's own. Whenever you feel unworthy or insignificant, remind yourself of this Scripture and allow it to affirm your value. He who has formed you knows you better than you know yourself. Let Him reveal more of Himself through you.

Zephaniah 3:17 — "The LORD your God is with you, the Mighty Warrior who saves. He will take great delight in you; in his love he will no longer rebuke you, but will rejoice over you with singing."

Practical application — Behold the image of God delighting in you and singing a love song to you. Allow this Scripture to reshape your perception of God's love, transforming it from a distant love to a gentle caress. God's love is not withdrawn and anemic; it is blanketing and robust. Whenever you doubt if He is near, attune your ear to the song He sings over you. He delights in you. Embrace this truth knowing that you are deeply cherished by the Almighty. Allow His love to draw you closer to Him, strengthening your faith and guiding your steps. Live with a heart full of gratitude in appreciation of the boundless love of the Father, knowing that you are forever held in His embrace.

Daily Unveiling

1. When you think about love, do you feel full or empty? Reflect on the reason for your feelings.

2. How do you define love? What are you using as the benchmark?

3. There are levels of love you cannot imagine. Pray this simple prayer: "God, exceed my expectations for love in my life."

Chapter 5

REMOVING BARRIERS

"When is it going to stop?" my son yelled as a pale shade of gray covered his face.

At that moment, my fear was confirmed. We had not waited an adequate amount of time between the chili cheese dogs and boarding the spinning teacups at the amusement park. Each 360-degree whirl around had me praying harder for the ride to end. Looking into the eyes of my son, I could see him fighting to hold it in. Fighting to withstand the relentless swirl of motion.

"Focus on Daddy standing at the gate," I said, to give him a fixed focal point.

Not a second too soon, we decelerated. The surroundings came back into focus and our little blue teacup settled in its place. My son could only manage a few steps off the ride before he literally lost his lunch. The release didn't happen during the spin; it came in the grounding. What's inside often comes up and out in the grounding.

Have you ever felt like you were caught in a cycle? Life spinning outside of your control. The scenes are blurry as one year turns into another. Time slows down. The same scenes repeat as you go through the motions of your life. Everything looks the same on the outside, but you feel an internal shift. Your external can be fixed even as you transform within.

The feelings and thoughts emerging from the inside can be illuminating but also disorienting. Processing inharmonious feelings requires that you evaluate what you have consumed and embrace your ability to determine when something needs to be purged from your system. As you ground yourself in the truth of God's Word, errant beliefs may come up in the spin that need to be expelled.

The innermost parts of who we are, including our desires, motivations, and beliefs about ourselves and the world, greatly impact our ability to enjoy life. Satisfaction begins on the inside. How you think and feel converges to construct your belief system. Along the way, we encounter various mindset hurdles and limiting patterns of belief. These self-sabotaging thoughts, which lead to behaviors, threaten to keep us from breaking free from negative cycles in our lives. Despite our desire to be different, we start each day thinking, feeling, and behaving the same way we did the day before.

The Spin Cycle

Have you ever wondered why a person can be so accomplished in one area but continue doing things that are obviously counterproductive in other areas? Why someone might be drawn to unhealthy foods, unwise spending, or dysfunctional relationships? What is driving these cycles of self-sabotage? Why are some of us chronically late to appointments, hiding bags of chips in the pantry, maxing out credit cards, or running from opportunities that stretch us? Why can't we stop these unproductive patterns even when we are trying hard to change? The result of our failure to change is shame about our shortcomings.

At one point in my life, I adopted a belief that if something good happened to me there had to be something bad coming close on its heels. This was not an untested idea but a reality I walked in. In my experience, periods of victory and celebration were often followed closely by struggle and difficulty. If I received a bonus at work, the dryer would break and I'd have to spend the bonus to replace it. If a great opportunity came my way, I'd get sick the week of the event. When you see something happen repeatedly, you start to believe that pattern is your reality. Faith in what is possible (through God) is replaced by faith in what is probable. This flawed faith isn't rooted in I AM but in I. Misplacing your faith in this way disconnects you from God and others and brings shame.

Shame functions at its highest capacity in isolation. It feeds on secrecy and empowers many of the destructive cycles we face. To avoid embarrassment, we only attempt what we believe we can accomplish in our own strength. We stay within the walls of our abilities and resist the support we need to remove the barriers in our way. Cycle breaking is messy work. Freedom does not come through individual effort alone. None of us has the power to defeat shame on our own. We need God's help. No amount of intellect and willpower will accomplish a finished work of inner transformation without a divine intervention.

Life is full of cycles. Some cycles are pleasant and desired like the cycles of the seasons and their accompanying holidays or the cycles of maturation that bring new experiences and expanded opportunities. Other cycles, such as debt, addiction, anger, or depression, cause fear and pain. As humans, we crave comfort and find it in patterns. It doesn't matter if the pattern is a healthy one or an unhealthy one, we just want to stop spinning and settle into a familiar groove. It's how our brains are designed. We want the comfort of knowing what is coming at the next turn, even if what's coming is not what we desire. We crave the peace that comes with knowing.

> No amount of intellect and willpower
> will accomplish a finished work of inner
> transformation without a divine intervention.

Before too long, however, we can find ourselves caught in an endless cycle of repeated unwanted habits that are hard to break. At times freedom from these compulsions may seem impossible. I can't count the number of times I have moved through a negative cycle of guilt and shame. I make promises to myself to exercise daily, gossip less, and connect with my kids more, but my good intentions are kicked out in the spin of unexpected schedule changes and juicy tea spilled once again. I tell myself I will make a different decision next time, only to do it again and repeat the cycle. When you've broken promises to yourself over and over, you eventually get to a point where you don't trust what you say about yourself. In those fleeting moments when your inner confidence arises to tell you who you are, you hear the echo of the voices in the cycle yelling, "Liar!"

Self-sabotage grows like a weed—at first unnoticed—in the field of your subconscious. It eventually undermines your confidence and prevents you from accomplishing all you're capable of achieving. Self-sabotage occurs when you do the opposite of what you should do without being fully aware of the reason behind your continued engagement in a destructive cycle. It is the accuser inside of you yelling, "Liar!" and pointing to your cycles as evidence and proof of your failure.

If you don't attend to the destructive cycles in your life, you'll likely not only repeat them but also teach them to your children and others in your life. Be a cycle breaker. Put an end to dysfunctional patterns before they sabotage you or your loved ones.

What's Keeping You

Most destructive cycles have hidden rewards that cause us to rejoin the spin cycle. We keep returning to the dysfunction for a tangible reason. Whether our cycle involves an addiction, a negative relationship, or a self-sabotaging behavior, you must realize there are likely alluring factors drawing you back to these harmful patterns. These rewards may not be immediately obvious. But upon closer inspection, they reveal themselves as faulty coping mechanisms that provide relief in the form of survival or avoidance. A temporary sense of relief can come from a feeling of control, familiarity, and comfort. For example, someone caught in the cycle of substance abuse may experience satisfaction or escape from their pain, temporarily masking deeper emotional wounds. They experience the reward of pain avoidance but at the great expense of healing.

The rewards attached to these cycles often serve as a shield against confronting uncomfortable truths or facing the challenge of change.

These rewards can also reinforce the cycle by creating a sense of dependency. Over time, what initially seemed like a coping mechanism can evolve into a self-perpetuating cycle, spinning you in an endless loop of destructive behavior.

Tearing down the barrier that prevents us from overcoming destructive cycles involves beholding the mercy of God. In Him, our emotions and desires find a place to rest as we accept His compassion toward our human condition. Leaving behind damaging patterns requires pulling down the veil on our motivations and triggers and understanding the rewards we seek and why we seek them. To break free from destructive cycles, we must be willing to confront uncomfortable truths, embrace vulnerability, and cultivate new patterns. As we recognize the hidden rewards that motivate us, we can begin to break free from their toxic grip on our lives.

Understanding and accepting God's mercy gives us strength to dismantle our negative patterns and go deep to uncover the soul wounds fueling our cycles. This process of self-discovery opens the pathway to healing and assures us we are not alone in our struggles. We can lean into God, relinquishing false rewards and trusting Him to dismantle the scaffolding of our destructive patterns. He alone can replace our rickety structures with the sure stronghold of His unfailing love and mercy. In this sacred journey of soul-deep restoration, we emerge redeemed, strengthened, and empowered to embrace a life of fulfillment and joyful satisfaction.

His mercy embraces us and gives us the courage to confront uncomfortable truths, such as a dependence on food, alcohol, substances, or sex to fill the emptiness we feel inside. Some of these uncomfortable truths surround how we treat others, including those closest to us. Maybe we put others down because we feel bad about ourselves. Perhaps we respond in anger because we are angry about something that has happened to us. As we surrender our vices and hidden rewards, we can break free from the chains of our destructive cycles. As you take steps toward I AM and away from I, you will begin to behold Him as the breaker liberating you from the bondage of your past and empowering you to walk in the fullness of Him.

As we surrender to the mercy of God, we are invited into a covenant relationship where His grace overshadows our human effort. It's a sacred collaboration where our willingness to repent aligns with His infinite compassion and power to save. In this dance of redemption and restoration, our need for mercy is met with His outstretched arm as if He were saying, "May I have this dance?" Now allow the truth of Scripture to wash over you, reminding you of His mercy and grace that tear down mindset barriers and destructive cycles and make all things possible.

Behold the Mercy of God

Ephesians 2:4–5 — "But because of his great love for us, God, who is rich in mercy, made us alive with Christ even when we were dead in transgressions—it is by grace you have been saved."

Practical application — Behold the depth of God's mercy in the gift of salvation through Jesus Christ. Each day, behold the enormity of this gift, which transcends all transgressions—past, present, and future—and allow this knowledge to fill you with gratitude. Let the reality of God's mercy knock down the walls keeping you distant from Him. Soak in the nearness of His presence, knowing that through Christ, you are offered forgiveness and eternal life.

Titus 3:5 — "He saved us, not because of righteous things we had done, but because of his mercy. He saved us through the washing of rebirth and renewal by the Holy Spirit."

Practical application — Behold the transformative power of God's mercy to overcome every destructive cycle and bring renewal. Take to heart that it is not your own righteousness that saves you, but God's great mercy made available to you through Jesus. Surrender yourself to the work of the Holy Spirit, allowing Him to wash away your sinful desires and renew you from within. Trust this process of spiritual rebirth and renewal, accepting God's mercy to continually transform you into the likeness of Christ.

Psalm 51:1–2 — "Have mercy on me, O God, according to your unfailing love; according to your great compassion blot out my transgressions. Wash away all my iniquity and cleanse me from my sin."

Practical application — Behold your heart's cry for mercy as you fix your gaze on the unfailing love and compassion of God. Acknowledge your need for His cleansing. Deliberately turn your heart toward Him, expecting His loving, purposeful restoration in your life. As you behold Him, shame will fail to keep you barricaded behind walls of guilt. Repentance tears down the barriers to restoration. Invite God to step into your spin cycles. Ask Him to purify your heart. Allow His mercy to bring forth the inner healing you seek.

Daily Unveiling

1. Are there any negative cycles you find repeating in your life, work, or family?

2. What are the hidden rewards of the cycle or pattern of behavior?

3. Destructive cycles can be redeemed and restored. Pray this simple prayer: "God, I receive Your mercy."

Chapter 6

THE UNRAVELED HEART

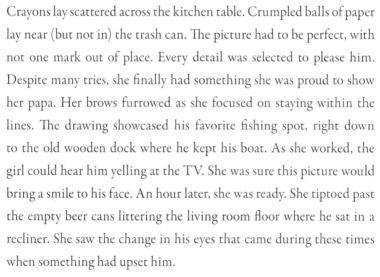

Crayons lay scattered across the kitchen table. Crumpled balls of paper lay near (but not in) the trash can. The picture had to be perfect, with not one mark out of place. Every detail was selected to please him. Despite many tries, she finally had something she was proud to show her papa. Her brows furrowed as she focused on staying within the lines. The drawing showcased his favorite fishing spot, right down to the old wooden dock where he kept his boat. As she worked, the girl could hear him yelling at the TV. She was sure this picture would bring a smile to his face. An hour later, she was ready. She tiptoed past the empty beer cans littering the living room floor where he sat in a recliner. She saw the change in his eyes that came during these times when something had upset him.

Still, she approached. "Papa," she asked timidly, "can I show you something?"

"What do you want now?" he barked.

"Nothing, Papa. I made you something," she answered, handing him the picture.

He glanced at the drawing before replying, "That's nice, but you are no artist."

And with that, he placed the picture face down on the coffee table before popping the top on another can.

"With each proposal, I fear someone will find out the truth," said my friend, a graphic designer. "I'm no artist," she admitted after sharing her story. "Every time I submit a new project, I see that picture face down on the table. It's a memory etched into my heart."

I ached for my friend. Despite having a very different experience with my father, I related to her current struggle. Words have power. Statements from those we love and admire become the seeds of our imagination and impact our belief in what is possible. Those seeds can either grow into buds of confidence or vines of insecurity. Each bud blossoms into something beautiful and each vine wraps a little tighter around our hearts, choking out our dreams.

In Stephen Covey's *The 7 Habits of Highly Effective People*, he states, "Begin with the end in mind." This requires you to transform your thoughts and the words you speak to yourself to match the results you desire. In doing so, the results become part of the motivation that compels you to keep going when things get hard. Jesus models this principle beautifully. Hebrews 12:2 encourages us to follow His example: "looking unto Jesus, the author and finisher of our faith, who for the joy that was set before Him endured the cross, despising the shame, and has sat down at the right hand of the throne of God" (NKJV).

Jesus had the end in mind—the joy set before Him. He endured physical and emotional abuse at the hands of His accusers. He persisted through betrayal when His closest friends became foes. He experienced pain so deeply, His family, helpless, could only stand in the shadows interceding for God to intervene. The path to securing our eternal redemption was not easy. It was unbelievably brutal. It bruised His body, tore at His emotions, and attacked His identity. What pain has bruised your body, torn at your emotions, and attacked your identity? What wounds have been etched on your heart?

As a physician, I've seen some really interesting physical heart malformations—from hearts with extra valves to vessels on the wrong side of the body. You might assume these heart conditions would be fatal, but in many cases these individuals are able to survive them. Often, surgery is required to correct what is out of place. In a similar way, negative emotions and past trauma can cause injury and damage to your heart. But healing is possible. With the right care, you can overcome spiritual and emotional heart conditions.

Everything you have encountered in your life has affected your heart, an innermost part of your being. Those times when your best efforts were not enough. The occasions when your love was not returned. The moments when you cried happy tears on your wedding day or the birth of a child. The times you cried tears of anguish for the death of a loved one or because of a failed relationship.

Every joy, every sorrow, every success, and every failure has shaped your heart. In some cases, the emotional effect was a soft caress that soothed the longing and filled a need. In other instances, the impact was sharp as a knife, tearing your peace to shreds and destroying your ability to trust. In the wake of such pain, you applied bandages, which may have not allowed the wounds to fully heal. Of all the characteristics of the heart, the quality I appreciate the most is its resilience. Our hearts fight to live. When they are wounded, they mend and persevere. Our hearts can bear the impact of our tragic experiences and survive, even emerging stronger than before.

Proverbs 4:23 cautions, "Keep your heart with all vigilance, for from it flow the springs of life" (ESV). This spring is the fountain from which being known flows. Being known is the river that feeds our compassion, desires, dreams, creativity, and endurance. As much as I love this Scripture, I have not always done a great job at applying it to my life. I have left my heart unguarded. In a desire to fit in, I have trusted people who were not trustworthy. In a longing for connection, I have subjected my heart to unhealthy situations and relationships. I have not always stewarded my heart well and the resulting wounds have required a lot of bandaging. I am thankful God is close to the brokenhearted and binds up their wounds (Ps. 147:3). Those times of intensive healing are needed to make it through grief, betrayal, abuse, and abandonment. But while God binds up your wounds, He does not want your spirit to remain bound. He came so you could be free. His renewal allows you to freely express the spring of life within your heart. His love frees you to embrace the many aspects of beholding, becoming, and belonging.

Dealing with Trauma

God yearns to mend the broken places in your heart. He will touch the places where trauma entered and patiently dress each unhealed wound from your past. Identity cannot thrive where trauma dominates—the two refuse to coexist in a healthy balance. Trauma stifles identity and causes gifted people to refrain from using their gift. Pain quiets voices that differ from the status quo and halts pioneers and innovators in their tracks. Unhealed trauma is the bully of the soul, contaminating the body and attempting to crush the spirit. The pain screams louder than positive affirmations, good intentions, and sometimes even faith. Trauma's goal is to rule the body and prevent any new opportunities for pain. In its inadequate attempt at self-protection, it creates greater dysfunction by suppressing identity and initiating an assault against being fully known.

Trauma skews truth. It distorts how you think about yourself, how you relate to others, how you interpret life, and how you perceive situations. When you were in the middle of trauma, much of your energy and time was spent on survival. For example, a child entrenched in the foster care system is not worrying about the future. His focus is on his current need. A mother in the middle of a divorce is not evaluating her heart's desires. She's trying to keep it all together for her kids. In times of emotional distress, the heart does not allow itself to expend its limited resources on trivial things like dreams, desires, and ambitions. What use do these have when you are trying to make it through just one more day? However, once you emerge from the storm, it is time to heal and recover.

Trauma is a bully. As with any bully, if you want the torment to stop, you must face your aggressor directly. If you experienced childhood trauma, understand that the wounds were inflicted during a critical stage of emotional development. Whether your trauma was the emotional distress of being raised by an alcoholic parent or what you consider to be run-of-the-mill family dysfunction, both types of trauma can have residual effects. Be patient with yourself. Healing occurs in stages. Maybe you have heard the phrase "Time heals all wounds." While this is not necessarily true—healing requires more than the passing of time—it does take time to process through the pain. You may also need a licensed mental health expert to guide you on your journey. Although difficult, the journey of healing is worth embarking on. As you behold a healing God and allow Him to bind up your wounds, you will learn more about who you are and about your God-given identity.

The Developmental Assets Framework[1] reveals why the things that happen in childhood impact our identities and describes "positive identity" as having the following four characteristics:

1. A sense of personal control over what happens to you.
2. A sense of self-esteem.
3. A sense of purpose.
4. A positive outlook on the future.

These traits should be cultivated during adolescence, which is when the true search for one's individual identity begins. Unfortunately, the nurturing of these characteristics by parents or caregivers doesn't always occur. Some children, then, are left to figure it out for themselves apart from that support because those who raised them were still navigating their own identity journey. So, some stumble along, with their hearts taking a few bumps along the way.

Traumatic experiences are not limited to childhood either. From sexual trauma during college to emotional trauma in a relationship to spiritual trauma from abusive church leaders, pain invades our lives in many ways. These situations can cause you to assume a trauma identity—you and the trauma become one. You become defined by what you have experienced and may fail to see aspects of yourself apart from past pain. Instead of recognizing your gifts and talents and tuning into your desires, you are dominated by the suffering you've experienced. Any gifts not associated with the trauma are locked away. Any talents that push back against the trauma are silenced. The pain rules above all desires. It becomes sovereign and dictates the story of your life.

Even if you have not faced significant trauma, each of us has sustained emotional damage of some kind. The grief of losing a loved one. Bouts of anxiety following a car accident. Negative self-talk in response to someone's careless words or hurtful labels. Few of us can get through a single day without reminders of pain, hurt, and disappointments we have experienced. Numerous studies confirm that trauma, even in small doses, can impact positive identity development and destabilize existing identity.[2]

While the scientific community has documented the negative lifelong effects of trauma many suffer, as believers we are not limited by statistics. We are not as those who have no hope because we recognize God's ability to step into the places where science is limited. While science observes and classifies the natural order, there is also a spiritual order that can supersede the physical. Both have a place and both are good. Just as you would call a doctor or therapist to enlist their help on your healing journey, the spiritual Healer also awaits an invitation. Spiritual healing prioritizes the beholding of God through a willingness to be present with Him.

Healing requires your participation, your yielded yes. Yes to the process. Yes to the messiness. Yes to the stretching. Yes to the unknown. Yes to help. Yes to support. Yes to beholding God's intervention. The healing begins with your yes. As you yield your need to understand and have all the answers, you open the door for God to enter the situation.

This is an unraveling process as God gently unties the knots and removes the bandages—insufficient coping mechanisms—that helped you survive. This transformative journey leads you away from your trauma identity and toward being fully known. It invites the question "Who am I now?" You cannot return to the person you were before. You have flipped the page to a new chapter of your life. The trauma has not disappeared. You still experienced it. Even after you reach a place of freedom, there will be times when the memory of your enslaved self comes rushing to the forefront of your mind. Triggers will set off a battery of neurophysiological responses in your body. A smell will remind you of the place where you were violated. A name will cause the hairs on your arm to stand at attention. A memory will leave you crying in the corner. There will be times when the pain comes back and crashes over you. And you will stand, rooted in the process of healing and clinging to the knowledge that you are not the trauma. The pain is not your identity, and in this new place of becoming, you will become familiar with the parts of your identity that have been hiding behind the walls you have erected to protect your heart. These emerging parts of your identity are stronger than you know and more capable than you can imagine. They have been waiting to ascend out of darkness and learn how to walk in the light.

> There will be times when the pain comes back and crashes over you. And you will stand, rooted in the process of healing and clinging to the knowledge that you are not the trauma.

For most of us, healing comes in waves and splashes—big breakthroughs followed by calm seasons that give way to tiny heart stirrings that ignite personal revival. Each healing journey is an adventure. Resist the trap of shame and feelings of failure that will try to stop you. God can heal you overnight, but my experience has been He often takes a gentler, slower approach. He gives you opportunities to practice healthy boundaries and self-disclosure with others over time. He lets you see the scars behind the bandages. He gives you time to appreciate the beauty of your healing heart. He extends the grace you need to see yourself scarred yet utterly lovely. He provides you with the freedom to explore, imagine, erase, and allow Him to rewrite the story of your trauma identity. Not on the other side of trauma. There is no other side. It is a part of you. But he endows you with a new narrative in which you openly share who you are now—scars and all. This new sense of identity adds rather than subtracts. Let all of it come through—your natural experiences, your pain, and your redeemed spiritual understanding. Welcome the truth of the trauma and the truth of who you are in Christ. The only way to be free is to allow it to become a redeemed part of your identity.

I've observed this in the life of a woman who, for years, lived the trauma of domestic violence. Once free from her abuser, she found it difficult to acclimate back into a normal way of living. Her experience affected every aspect of her life and her identity. With the help of some caring friends, who took her in and patiently cared for her physical, emotional, and spiritual needs, she was able to be restored. By beholding God and accepting His healing process, she gained an understanding of her identity in Christ and her identity as a voice for the voiceless. This new narrative allows her to offer inside knowledge about domestic violence to help organizations desiring to be a part of the solution. Her new story includes both the trauma and the healing.

Behold the Comfort of God

Lamentations 3:22–23 — "Because of the LORD's great love we are not consumed, for his compassions never fail. They are new every morning; great is your faithfulness."

Practical application — Behold God's compassion at the dawning of each new day. Look for opportunities to witness God's faithfulness in your healing process. As the sun rises, it testifies of His commitment to you because His mercies are new every morning. Begin each day in thanksgiving. Let the awareness of Him shape your outlook, prompting you to linger a little longer in His presence.

Psalm 23:4 — "Even though I walk through the darkest valley, I will fear no evil, for you are with me; your rod and your staff, they comfort me."

Practical application — Behold the comforting presence of God in your pain. Instead of focusing on your fears, focus on His care. Do not allow despair to overtake you. Behold the Comforter coming alongside you. Lean on His strength and provision to sustain you through every trial and hardship. Find solace in knowing He is with you, leading you through the darkest valleys and bringing you safely to the other side. His comforting presence will bring peace to your soul and hope to your heart, knowing that He will never leave you nor forsake you.

Romans 8:28 — "And we know that in all things God works for the good of those who love him, who have been called according to his purpose."

Practical application — Behold the promise that God is able to bring something good out of every situation. Trauma is no exception. He remains sovereign in His ability to work all things together for your ultimate good. Accept the growth process of adversity and behold God using every experience to reveal His character to you. Choose to align your heart with God's. Feel how His heart beats for you, even when circumstances seem bleak. When faced with difficulty and dysfunction, behold God's omnipotence (endless power) and trust in His faithfulness to bring about deliverance. Exchange overwhelm for overcoming peace as you pray and inquire of His counsel. In the comfort of His presence, find healing for your brokenness and restoration for your spirit.

Daily Unveiling

1. Who were you before you experienced trauma? What were your interests, desires, and dreams prior to the traumatic experience?

2. What has trauma taken from you? Think of broad categories like "my childhood," "my sense of security," "my peace," or "my confidence."

3. Restoration is a process of rebuilding and renewing. It returns what has been taken. Pray this simple prayer: "Lord, I surrender my yielded yes to Your healing process."

Chapter 7

UNDIMINISHED POWER

I stood in my front yard wearing a ridiculous pair of cardboard glasses. On this day, God's awesomeness was on display in a special way through a total solar eclipse—a rare moment when the sun and the moon share space. Both acknowledge the hand of God in orchestrating their coming and going, and each bows in reverence to His sovereignty. When the day darkens as if it's night, a holy moment of God's omnipotence is on display. The temperature drops within minutes, birds scatter through the trees, and the woods come alive with the sounds of dusk in the middle of the day. I gazed into the sky, awed by the sounds of nature yielding to the moment.

The darkness was my permission to remove my protective eyewear. A deer wandering out of the woods startled me, disrupting the moment. It stood at the edge of the trees surrounding our property. This is a common occurrence in the evening on our wooded lot when everyone is inside, and the area is undisturbed by humans. Typically, deer are skittish and bolt at the sign of humans. But this doe seemed oblivious to my existence. She nibbled on the high grass, occasionally glancing up toward the sky. I, too, looked to the heavens. For a few minutes, it appeared the sun and the moon stood still. The darkness lingered. Evening rituals invaded the day. The boundaries were crossed. Creation bent its will to the Creator. Then, with the finality of the "Amen" at the end of a prayer, the sun and moon bid each other farewell and began to go their separate ways.

Routines and patterns are a natural part of our existence. Morning rolls in with the rising of the sun. The moon withdraws to rest. Fall gives way to winter. Spring meets its end as temperatures rise, ushering in summer. While centuries of scientific study have attempted to explain the unexplainable majesty of God's creation, it remains a work of beauty that provokes our awe and delight. The Psalmist wrote, "The heavens declare the glory of God; the skies proclaim the work of his hands" (Ps. 19:1). Nestled within the matrix of our DNA is an understanding of our smallness and His greatness. There is none like our God.

We see power displayed in various ways in our world. Teachers have the power to determine the grade you receive on an essay. The police have the power to give you a speeding ticket when your foot gets heavy on the pedal. Bosses have the power to hire and fire. Around tax season, it can feel like the IRS has power to control your money. As shown in these examples, power is synonymous with control, authority, and influence. These are certainly aspects of power. These words probably also come to mind when you think about powerful people in our world.

The power of God extends beyond our human understanding of power. God's power encompasses the capability, capacity, function, and potential of all of heaven. God's power cannot be diminished or taken away; it possesses stability and sustainability. Both words share the suffix *ability*. God's power has the ability to render all things possible in heaven and on earth. He is able to *sustain* and *make stable* whatever He desires.

In the Old Testament, we read about God's power "coming upon" certain individuals. For example, after Saul was appointed king, the prophet Samuel says, "The Spirit of the LORD will come powerfully upon you, and you will prophesy with them" (1 Sam. 10:6). In the book of Judges, we see that the power of God came on men like Gideon and Samson to do mighty deeds. In the New Testament we see a shift. Through the death and resurrection of Jesus, and the gift of the Holy Spirit, we have been given full access to God's wonder-working power. Acts 1:8a says, "But you will receive power when the Holy Spirit comes on you." Following Pentecost, the day the Holy Spirit descended on all believers, the power of God doesn't come upon us; it resides within us.

Spiritual Surge Protectors

Have you encountered moments where it feels as though the power of God is not flowing freely through you? It may feel like there are unseen gatekeepers or blockades inhibiting the full expression of His grace and transformative power in your life. This isn't all in your head. Even when we know the Lord, we can unwittingly be the cause of a diminished flow of His power. We may place limitations on the power God infuses in our lives, much like a spiritual surge protector.

Just as a surge protector regulates the amount of electrical current that reaches our electronic devices, we can have self-imposed restrictions that regulate the extent to which we allow God's power to manifest in our lives. These constraints can take various forms, such as doubt, fear, unforgiveness, pride, or self-reliance. Additionally, misconceptions about our worthiness and abilities, or our trust in God's ability to work through us, may impede the amount of spiritual power we have access to. While fear, doubt, and unforgiveness may initially serve to protect us from the pain or discomfort of allowing God to have His way with us, these ultimately hinder the full expression of His power in our lives.

Consider how a surge protector operates during a power surge: it absorbs excess energy to prevent damage to our electronic devices. Similarly, when faced with overwhelming challenges or blessings beyond our comprehension, we may instinctively dampen the full force of God's power. We fear the unknown or doubt our capacity to handle such immense divine intervention. In doing so, we limit the miraculous and delay breakthroughs God desires to bring forth in our lives.

Instead of diminishing the output of God's power by seeking to harness it, we must remove the barriers we've constructed and invite the full flow of His Holy Spirit power. We were created to access the unlimited power of God in our day-to-day lives. By surrendering our addiction to control and comfort, we open ourselves to the boundless possibilities of His supernatural ability and guidance. As we seek to understand and identify the things in our lives that block

God's power, our relationship with Him will deepen and we will experience His abundant life. We must discard our spiritual surge protector and instead allow the unbridled power of God to surge through our lives.

Experiencing God's power in this way requires that we employ regular practices that tear down what blocks spiritual electricity from flowing through our lives. The following habits will help you unlock greater power in your life:

Allow God to renew your mind. Romans 12:2 encourages us to "not conform to the pattern of this world, but be transformed by the renewing of your mind." Read God's Word and allow that steady stream of hope and possibility to replace negative mindsets, opening your mind to God's unlimited power.

Seek wisdom. Proverbs 4 reminds us that wisdom and understanding are two of the most valuable things to possess in this life (v. 7). Pray for wisdom, seek understanding, and listen to godly counsel from mature believers to gain clarity. Increased discernment will help you dismantle spiritual power blocks.

Cultivate humility. James 4:10 tells us, "Humble yourselves before the Lord, and he will lift you up." Pride can block God's power. It keeps you from submitting to His will and accepting His grace, because you believe you can handle it yourself. When you humble yourself before the Lord and admit to your powerlessness, He can fully enter the situation and show His strength in your weakness.

Guard your heart. We receive the following instruction from Proverbs 4:23: "Above all else, guard your heart, for everything you do flows from it." Spiritual surge protectors often originate from negative thought patterns, bitterness, unforgiveness, or sinful desires that entangle our hearts. When we cultivate a pure heart that's surrendered to God's truth, we create a place for the power of God to operate in and through us.

Seek God's kingdom first. In Matthew 6:33, Jesus urges, "But seek first his kingdom and his righteousness, and all these things will be given to you as well." When you seek God's priorities and righteousness above all else, you align yourself with His purposes and invite His power to show up in your circumstances in ways beyond your imagination.

Pray and fast. These disciplines are shown throughout Scripture to invite God's power into situations. Spiritual fasting is humbling yourself before God by choosing to deny yourself something you need or enjoy, such as food or social media, for a period of time. Believers are called to fast before making important decisions and to show repentance. Isaiah 58:6–11 also suggests fasting can include humbling yourself through acts of service like feeding the hungry and caring for the widow. Prayer and fasting have the power to move mountains and break through gates hindering your spiritual growth and intimacy with Him.

Cultivate community. Hebrews 10:24–25 tells us to "consider how we may spur one another on toward love and good deeds, not giving up meeting together … but encouraging one another." At the dinner table, share one thing you've learned in this book. Arrange a coffee date with a friend or join a small group. Surrounding yourself with a supportive community of believers who can provide accountability, encouragement, and prayer support can help you overcome spiritual surge protectors and walk in the fullness of God's power and purpose.

Practice gratitude. In 1 Thessalonians 5:18, we're encouraged to "give thanks in all circumstances; for this is God's will for you in Christ Jesus." Cultivating an attitude of gratitude helps you shift focus from your limitations to God's abundance, enabling you to receive more of His blessings and power.

God's power knows no limits. God's strength and might remain undiminished and readily available. Understanding the concept of spiritual surge protectors offers profound insight into how we can inadvertently limit the flow of the power of God in our lives. By recognizing our self-imposed restriction, we can take intentional steps to demolish them through prayer, study of His Word, humility, and community. As we surrender these hindrances and cultivate a heart that is rooted in faith, gratitude, and obedience, we open ourselves to the unlimited power that can do more than we ask or imagine (Eph. 3:20).

Build an Altar

The Holy Spirit's transformative work in us releases the unrestricted flow of God's power into every facet of our lives. As we relinquish the things holding us back, we invite His superior ability to energize us when our natural ability comes to an end and can become human conduits of His power on earth. This isn't a passive surrender but an active one, a willing choice to partner with God in the miraculous and defer to His supernatural ways. We yield the right of way to His power in us, allowing it to flow according to His will and desires.

Acceptance of God's power in your life begins with an altar where you lay an offering—a symbolic act of surrendering your own efforts to God. The act of giving up control paves the way for God's divine power to work in your life. These altars are places where the fire of God's sovereignty burns away the spiritual surge protectors we have in place.

One significant offering is **humility**. When you humble yourself before God, acknowledging your limitations and inadequacies, you make room for His power to show up in your life. Humility disarms the spiritual surge protector of pride, which often prevents us from fully trusting that God's way is best. By bowing before Him in humility, you position yourself to receive His grace and direction.

Another crucial offering is **obedience**. When you choose to obey God's commands and promptings, even when they seem counterintuitive or challenging, you demonstrate your trust in His authority. Obedience disarms the spiritual surge protector of self-reliance, as you learn to live righteously and depend wholly on God's provision. As you lay your will on the altar of obedience, God's power is unleashed in your life, enabling you to accomplish His purposes and experience His peace and goodness beyond measure.

A third offering is **forgiveness**. When you extend forgiveness to those who have wronged you, you allow the Lord to disarm the spiritual surge protectors of bitterness and resentment. Forgiveness is a powerful act of surrender and reflects your understanding of His mercy toward you. As you forgive others, you open yourself to receive God's forgiveness and experience the liberating power of His redeeming love.

The fourth offering is **surrender**. As you willingly surrender your plans, desires, and ambitions to God, you disarm the spiritual surge protector of control. Yielding to a powerful God shines light on our illusion of self-sufficiency as we entrust our days entirely to God's care. As you lay down your agenda on the altar of surrender, you welcome God to work in and through you according to His perfect will.

The final crucial offering is **worship**. When you lift your voice in praise and adoration, declaring God's greatness and majesty, you align with all creation, which praises Him. Worship disarms doubt. It focuses your attention on God's sufficiency instead of your circumstances. As you exalt God above all through your offering of worship, His power is magnified, bringing the clarity, strength, and renewed faith you need to face any challenge.

God's power transcends human limitations. Each of the five offerings mentioned represents a sacred space where we lay down our inadequacy. Approach them with a posture of reverence and expectancy, knowing the God of heaven is listening and caring for you. These places of surrender serve as sanctuaries where our weaknesses are met with His strength, our doubts with His truth, and our brokenness with His healing touch. May we continually cultivate hearts of humility, obedience, forgiveness, surrender, and worship. Let's cease striving in our own strength and behold the power of God. He delights to work wonders in and through you.

Behold the Power of God

Psalm 62:11–12 — "One thing God has spoken, two things I have heard: 'Power belongs to you, God, and with you, Lord, is unfailing love.'"

Practical application: Behold the sovereignty and power of God as the ultimate authority over all things. Trust in His strength and ability to accomplish His purposes on the earth and in your life. Surrender your fears and anxieties in faith, believing God holds all power in His hands. Rely on His might to overcome obstacles and challenges, confident that nothing is impossible for Him.

Jeremiah 32:17 — "Ah, Sovereign LORD, you have made the heavens and the earth by your great power and outstretched arm. Nothing is too hard for you."

Practical application — Behold the limitless potential of God's power to accomplish whatever He bids. Lift your prayers with boldness and faith, knowing God is able to do more than what your wildest imagination can conceive. Trust in His ability to intervene in any situation to bring about a miraculous breakthrough. Walk confidently, knowing nothing can stand against the power of God working on your behalf.

Ephesians 3:20 — "Now to him who is able to do immeasurably more than all we ask or imagine, according to his power that is at work within us."

Practical application — Behold the surpassing greatness of God's power, which is at work within you. Lean into His strength and ability, knowing it empowers you to be a victorious overcomer. Surrender your limitations and weaknesses to Him, allowing His power to be made perfect in your weakness. Walk in boldness, trusting He is sufficient for anything you face.

Daily Unveiling

1. What spiritual surge protectors are affecting how you experience God's power—pride, self-reliance, bitterness, resentment, control, doubts, etc.?

2. Which altar is the Holy Spirit inviting you to build—humility, obedience, forgiveness, surrender, worship?

3. Power flows from the greater to the lesser, from the Almighty to the humble vessel. Pray this simple prayer: "God, move with power in my life."

Chapter 8

UNRIVALED CAPACITY

Imagine waking up to the soft glow of dawn seeping through your curtains, and the gentle chirping of birds greeting the new day. As you stretch and yawn, you realize with a jolt of gratitude that you've been granted another day of life. In this simple act of waking up each morning, God's grace is revealed through the gift of a fresh start, a new opportunity to experience His goodness and faithfulness. It's in the quiet moments of dawn, with the world still asleep and the day full of possibilities, that His grace whispers, "I am with you, and I will guide you through the day ahead."

Now turn your thoughts to the mundane task of preparing breakfast—cracking eggs into a sizzling skillet, breathing in the aroma of freshly brewed coffee that wafts through the kitchen. As you take a sip of your morning brew and savor the first bite of your meal, you pause to reflect on the abundance before you. In the simple act of providing sustenance for your body, God's grace is evident. The food and drink nourish you physically and remind you of His dependability. In the ordinary ritual of breakfast-making, with each ingredient a reminder of His abundant provision, He whispers, "I am the source of all good things; trust Me to supply your needs and be satisfied."

Picture yourself caught in the grind of rush-hour traffic. Horns honk and brake lights flash as you navigate the crowded street. Just as frustration begins to creep in, you glance out the window and glimpse a vibrant sunset painting the sky in hues of pink and gold. In this moment of calm amidst chaos, God's grace is revealed in the reminder of His creativity and majesty. This glimpse of His glory transcends the grittiness of life. In the unexpected beauty of a sunset at the end of a busy day, His grace whispers, "I am present in your busyness; find Me in the beauty around you and rest in My presence."

These everyday examples are tangible reminders that God's grace permeates every moment of your life, even the most mundane. They are snapshots of God beholding you. He is mindful of your daily routines and invites you to pause and recognize His presence in the ordinary moments. From the simplicity of a sunrise to the chaos of rush-hour traffic, God's grace surrounds us, offering glimpses of His character if we have eyes to see and hearts to perceive.

As we reflect on these everyday encounters with grace, we begin to recognize that God's grace extends far beyond what we can comprehend, though there is much evidence of it. Grace is not confined to grand gestures or dramatic displays but reveals itself in the quiet whispers of dawn, the aroma of breakfast, and the beauty of a sunset. As your busy life unfolds, open your heart to receive God's grace in all its forms. Let your striving draw you closer to the One who reveals His love to you in countless ways, both big and small.

Five Graces to Behold

Grace is God's unmerited favor and goodness toward us. God demonstrates His grace in a variety of ways, each one a testament to His unrivaled capacity. One significant way He shows His grace, and by far the greatest, is through the gift of salvation, freely offered to all who believe in His Son, Jesus Christ. Ephesians 2:8–9 reminds us, "For it is by grace you have been saved, through faith—and this is not from yourselves, it is the gift of God—not by works, so that no one can boast." Through the sacrifice of Jesus on the cross, God extends His grace to us, forgiving our sins and granting us eternal life.

Another way God reveals His grace is through His provision and supply. In Matthew 6:26, Jesus says, "Look at the birds of the air; they do not sow or reap or store away in barns, and yet your heavenly Father feeds them. Are you not much more valuable than they?" God's grace is evident in the way He meets our needs, providing for us physically, emotionally, and spiritually. Even in times of scarcity or uncertainty, you can trust His ability to provide and care for you.

God also reveals His grace through His mercy and compassion toward us. Lamentations 3:22–23 declares, "Because of the LORD's great love we are not consumed, for his compassions never fail. They are new every morning; great is your faithfulness." Despite our failures and shortcomings, God extends His mercy to us, offering forgiveness and second chances. His compassion knows no bounds, and His grace covers us like a protective shield, guarding us from the eternal consequences of our sins.

His grace is also revealed through the gift of His Word, serving as a source of strength and encouragement. Psalm 119:105 declares, "Your word is a lamp for my feet, a light on my path." In the pages of

Scripture, we find wisdom, comfort, and assurance. His Word speaks truth into our lives, guiding us through the trials we face, and reminding us of His promises.

Lastly, God reveals His grace through the gift of His Holy Spirit, who dwells within all who have accepted Jesus as Savior, empowering us to live lives that honor and glorify Him. Jesus promised His disciples, "And I will ask the Father, and he will give you another advocate to help you and be with you forever—the Spirit of truth. The world cannot accept him, because it neither sees him nor knows him. But you know him, for he lives with you and will be in you" (John 14:16–17). The Holy Spirit equips us with the gifts and fruit necessary to fulfill God's purposes for our lives, while guiding us in paths of righteousness and leading us into deeper intimacy with our heavenly Father.

As we contemplate the many ways in which God reveals His grace to us, we are invited into a deeper understanding of His unrivaled capacity to love and bless His children. The word *unrivaled* encapsulates the idea of the unparalleled nature of God. He surpasses all other forms of existence. He stands alone in magnitude and scope, extending beyond our comprehension. There is no one and nothing with which to compare Him. His capacity knows no bounds, reaching into every corner of our existence and meeting us exactly where we are.

Blessed Indeed

In the depths of our hearts lies a longing for more—more love, more joy, more peace, more kindness, more goodness. Yet, to ask God for more is to invite expansion beyond the known. It's a prayer that requires courage, because if He grants our request, we will be stretched beyond what we thought possible. This is the by-product of a lifestyle of beholding—daily noticing God everywhere infiltrates every part of your life. You dare to utter the scary prayers, leaning on your Beloved for support. Then you prepare to witness the unrivaled capacity of God.

In this mindset, you count it a blessing to confront your fears and insecurities, recognizing true growth often comes through discomfort. You surrender your limitations and open yourself to the infinite possibilities that await when you trust in God's provision and guidance. With each prayer for more, you embrace the process of stepping out of your comfort zone. You dive headfirst into the unknown, confident in the One who knows you.

In asking for more love, we recognize our need to love others as God loves us—unconditionally and sacrificially. We seek to embody the type of love that knows no bounds, extending grace and compassion to the people we encounter. As God pours His love into our hearts, we discover a reservoir of loving-kindness that overflows, touching lives and comforting hearts in profound ways.

In praying for more joy, we relinquish the shackles of discontentment and embrace a spirit of gratitude and celebration. We choose to find satisfaction in the simple pleasures of life, knowing that true happiness is found in the presence of God and the richness of His blessings. As we abide in Him, a joyful God, our joy becomes contagious, illuminating the darkness and drawing others into the warmth of His light.

With each request for more peace, we confront the chaos and turmoil of the world around us, anchoring ourselves in the unshakable, soul-deep tranquility that comes from knowing God. We surrender our anxieties and fears, trusting His sovereignty and resting in the assurance that He holds all things securely in His hands. During life's storms, we find refuge in His peace that surpasses understanding and anchors our emotions.

Praying for more kindness opens our hearts to the needs of those around us, prompting us to seek opportunities to extend compassion and generosity. We strive to emulate the kindness of our heavenly Father, who lavishes His compassion on us without measure. Through small and large acts of kindness, we become vessels of His love, shining brightly into a world in need of mercy and compassion.

In asking for more goodness, we pursue holiness and righteousness that comes from God. We give Him permission to refine and purify our hearts as we, compelled by His love, strive to align our thoughts, words, and actions with His perfect will. In all of this, we recognize true goodness flows from a life surrendered to Him. As we walk in obedience and integrity, we bear witness to the power of God's goodness at work within us.

Through these scary prayers, we discover our Father's unrivaled capacity to do more in and through us. He exceeds our expectations. We are left to marvel at His boundless love, infinite joy, profound peace, unfailing kindness, and unending goodness. In stretching our capacity, we find ourselves drawn ever closer to gaze at our Beloved.

Exodus 6:2–3 says, "Then God spoke further to Moses and said to him, 'I am the LORD. I appeared to Abraham, to Isaac, and to Jacob (Israel) as God Almighty [El Shaddai], but by My name, LORD, I did not make Myself known to them [in acts and great miracles]'" (AMP).

How much of God's capacity has been made known to you?

The name of God as "El Shaddai" holds profound significance in understanding His unrivaled capacity. It is one of the ancient Hebrew names for God, often translated as "God Almighty" or "God of the Mountains."[1] This name speaks to God's overwhelming power to meet all of our needs and overcome any obstacle or challenge we may face. Just as mountains stand as symbols of strength and immovability, so, also, does God's power as El Shaddai remain steadfast and unshakable. He possesses capacity beyond human comprehension, making Him capable of performing miracles and fulfilling His promises.

In Hebrew, the phrase "Shaddai" can also be interpreted as "breast," evoking imagery of a mother tenderly nursing her child or holding it close to her body. This meaning speaks to God's intimate care and maternal love for His children. It highlights His nurturing and protective nature. Just as a mother provides nourishment and sustenance to the infant at her breast, so, too, does God provide abundantly for His children. His love is nurturing and sustaining, like the milk that nourishes a newborn, flowing freely to meet every need and bring forth growth.

Consider God's maternal care for you and the nourishment He offers. Trust in His unrivaled capacity to meet your needs, protect you from harm, and bring forth new life. We can be at peace knowing we are cradled in the arms of the One who tenderly cares for us as a mother cares for her child. Heed the invitation of Psalm 91 to dwell in the secret place of the Most High and run under the refuge of His wing.

When we call upon God as El Shaddai, we are truly acting like His children, knowing that He desires to be needed by us and will be faithful to act on our behalf. This is the grace available to those willing to behold Him as both paternal and maternal, experiencing the fullness of His unrivaled capacity.

Behold the Grace of God

2 Corinthians 12:9–10 — "But he said to me, 'My grace is sufficient for you, for my power is made perfect in weakness.' Therefore I will boast all the more gladly about my weaknesses, so that Christ's power may rest on me. That is why, for Christ's sake, I delight in weaknesses, in insults, in hardships, in persecutions, in difficulties. For when I am weak, then I am strong."

Practical application — Behold God's sufficiency to uphold you in your weaknesses. Instead of trying to overcome in your own strength, rely on the power of Christ to work through your weakness. Cultivate a holy dependence on God, knowing that it is in your moments of greatest frailty that His strength is most prominently displayed. Rejoice in the opportunity for Him to get the glory.

Ephesians 2:8–9 — "For it is by grace you have been saved, through faith—and this is not from yourselves, it is the gift of God—not by works, so that no one can boast."

Practical application — Behold the gift of God's grace freely offered to all who believe. Salvation is not something we earn through our own efforts but rather a gracious gift from God. Lift a spirit of gratitude for God's unmerited favor toward you and let it fuel your devotion and adoration. Behold each day with a sense of awe and wonder at the depth of God's mercy, knowing it is through His grace that you are saved.

John 1:16 — "Out of his fullness we have all received grace in place of grace already given."

Practical application — Behold the abundant grace that flows from His fullness. Recognize every blessing and provision as the overflow of His grace. Behold in gratitude the divine favor you have received, knowing it is given without limit. Live each day with a heart full of thankfulness for the grace of God.

Daily Unveiling

1. Make a list of ten ways God has provided for your needs today.
2. Which of the five graces have you not been beholding in your life—salvation, provision and supply, mercy and compassion, God's Word, the Holy Spirit?
3. Grace is as essential to your existence as the blood flowing through your veins. Pray this simple prayer: "God, show me the sufficiency of Your grace."

Chapter 9

UNEXPLAINABLE EXPRESSION

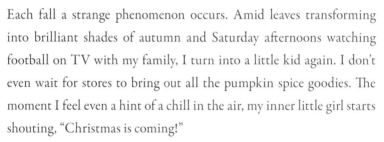

Each fall a strange phenomenon occurs. Amid leaves transforming into brilliant shades of autumn and Saturday afternoons watching football on TV with my family, I turn into a little kid again. I don't even wait for stores to bring out all the pumpkin spice goodies. The moment I feel even a hint of a chill in the air, my inner little girl starts shouting, "Christmas is coming!"

Everything about the Christmas season brings me joy: the colorful flashing lights, the sweet smell of gingerbread cookies, the increase in generosity and giving, and the expression of love toward all mankind. Jesus is a gift like no other—the light in the darkness, the sweet aroma of eternal life, the perfect selfless sacrifice, and the greatest manifestation of the Father's love. The thought of Him makes me want to cry and laugh uncontrollably at the same time. That's what Christmas does to me. It excites me and overwhelms me with the magnitude of the Gift. It leaves me feeling like a much-loved child. It provokes me to respond in gratitude and praise.

Love will do that to you. It will unsettle you in the best way possible. It will call you out of your self-made comforts. It will beckon you beyond your safety zone. It will take you farther than you would normally go. When love tears through your barrier of protection, your heart breaks open and releases what is inside with total disregard for logic and reason. Your heart beats to a different rhythm—the heartbeat of the One who created you in His image.

> This is what love does. It volunteers
> itself as the most valuable gift.

And while we are talking about beats, let's not forget the Christmas carols. Who doesn't love singing at the top of their lungs about peace, joy, and hope? One of my all-time favorites is "The Little Drummer Boy." I can't resist singing along as the song blasts through my car speakers. *I have no gift to bring... that's fit to give our King.* As is typical with my nerdy personality, my curiosity led me to research the origin of the song.

Jake Riley shares the following explanation in "The Meaning Behind the Song: The Little Drummer Boy (Carol of the Drum)":

> At its core, The Little Drummer Boy is a tale of
> humility, simplicity, and the power of offering what
> we have, no matter how small or insignificant it may

seem. The boy, lacking material gifts like the three wise men, plays his drum for the baby Jesus as his gift. This act of playing the drum represents the boy's desire to give the only thing he possesses—his talent and devotion. It symbolizes the purity and innocence of a child's heart, reminding us that we can all contribute something meaningful, regardless of our limitations.[1]

This is what love does. It volunteers itself as the most valuable gift.

The Gifts We Bring

What gift can you bring to the One who owns everything in creation? Even within the song, the little drummer boy offered his talent of playing as a gift. Where did that talent come from? Is there anything we possess outside of our Creator? Yes. God has given us the freedom to choose. This is the same free will Eve possessed to choose to listen to the serpent in the garden. It is the same free will Peter possessed to choose to step out of the boat onto the waters with Jesus. To choose and to refuse are both decisions and functions of the will.

The gifts we bring to God are the things within us—our hearts, our desires, and our will. These are our most valuable gifts. They are the places where our hope, significance, and validation reside. They are the idols of our generation. We no longer practice idolatry like the Israelites in the Old Testament, melting down our gold earrings and necklaces to make a shiny calf to worship. Our idols are more sophisticated and subtle. Status, stature, and stuff become the things we elevate in our hearts. They are the things we idolize, the things we believe will prove our worth. In all our striving we become disconnected from what fuels our heartbeat, disconnected from what brings us joy and satisfaction. A divide occurs between our inward longings and our outward actions.

At the start of each year, one of my favorite activities is creating a vision board. I do not consider myself to be a naturally crafty person; I must credit my friend Pat for unlocking that gene within me. During the first rest retreat we hosted, she insisted I participate in the craft time she had planned. I am all for a creative release, but glue guns and paint did not look like a fun time to me. Despite my reluctance, I decided I should be a good role model for the ladies attending the retreat and settled into a chair at a table stacked with magazines, my scissors in hand. I looked up a few hours later to find Pat snapping photos of me and laughing. "I knew you'd love it!" she said. I was one of the last women in the room to finish, as I had been fully engrossed in my vision.

Until that day, I had always considered myself to be someone who knew what she wanted. If someone had asked me, I could have rattled off my tidy list of desires. "I want to have a healthy, happy family. I want to have a fulfilling job. I want to be full of hope and joy." I knew how I wanted to feel. I could picture the results of what I desired. But I did not know what I desired. What I truly longed for was to have greater connections with my husband and sons, freedom to love people using my God-given talents, and the joy of knowing the fullness of God's love. Creating a vision board brought clarity to my desires and allowed me to see what was unseen and not immediately apparent. It also helped me to realize the limitations I placed on what was possible.

I had never seen firsthand the type of family closeness and connection I desired, so I set my bar low rather than allowing the Holy Spirit to raise my expectations.

Years later, I was asked to be the guest speaker at a women's ministry beach retreat. When I am preparing to speak at an event, I make it a point to connect with the host to hear that individual's heart and vision for the time. Though it's rare that an event planner is vague on details, I assume when it happens it may be she is still figuring them out herself. So, when this ministry leader told me, "I just want the women to understand how to rest," I didn't push any further. I would have probed more deeply if I had known how God would use that event to unearth my idols.

> Our idols are more sophisticated and subtle. Status, stature, and stuff become the things we elevate in our hearts.

I arrived at the beachside location hours before the opening session and was elated to find I had been given an oceanside room with an amazing view of the Gulf Shores. Out on the balcony, the sound of the waves crashing on the sand immediately whispered rest to my soul. By the first session, I was already feeling well rested. On my way into the banquet hall, I stopped at the event registration table and was handed a white bag with the word "Hineni" written in gold calligraphy. My fixation with enjoying the balcony view had me pressed for time, so I vowed to look up the word that night before I spoke the next morning to be sure I understood the theme of the retreat. I didn't want to appear unprepared and present a message not aligned with the event planner's vision. After all, her ministry was footing the bill for me to come, so I had a duty to please her, right?

Worship filled the banquet hall as feminine voices lifted their praise to God. The room was filled with holy anticipation. Women had left their safe spaces and traveled by air and road to seek God. There was a tangible pressure in the room to go further in the expression of their love for their King. The praise in the room quickened our hearts and seemed to bring heaven near. When the women's ministry leader went to the mic to share the opening message, the hair on my arms stood at attention.

"What will you bind to the altar?" were her opening words.

She read the story of Abraham from Genesis 22. In this passage, God asks Abraham to take his only son, Isaac, up on a mountain and offer him as a sacrifice. The request is shocking. You can imagine Abraham's emotions, considering God used the stars in the sky to construct Abraham's vision board of populating the earth with his offspring. How was that going to happen if his promised heir was dead?

Despite the conflict between the promise and the request, Abraham agrees and proceeds up the mountain to do what God requests. If you have ever seen a children's church rendition of this story, Isaac is often shown as a young child. However, many Bible scholars believe Isaac was a young man when this occurred. He was not likely a little boy Abraham could easily pick up to place on the altar, but, for visual purposes, more like my six-foot-tall athletic son. Not only would Isaac have had to climb onto the altar himself, he would have had to willingly stay still and not resist being bound to the altar.

Like Abraham and Isaac, we, too, must relinquish our wills to His. Giving our personal agendas back to the King is an act of faith, honor, and trust. Laying down our autonomy isn't a partial work but a complete one. All of our will is exchanged for His will to be done. It is a binding of every heart desire, every hope, every pull of the will to the altar until God is our only desire.

There is a beautiful song about this passage of Scripture called "Hineni (The Binding of Isaac)" on Sarah Liberman's *God of Miracles* album. These are a few of my favorite lines from the song:

> When you bound me
> You found me
> (Now fear doesn't hold me)
> Hineni, Hineni

The women's ministry leader, who I'll call Jan, relieved my need to research the word *hineni* as she led us in a deep study of it that night. In Hebrew the word means, "Here I am." After the binding to the altar, after the gift-giving, we can then say, "Here I am, God! Here I am unchained to fear. Here I am free from the battle of my will versus Your will. Here I am, a vessel available to You."

Jan played the song three times. The first time she shared the theatrical video that accompanies it. I watched as Abraham notified Sarah of God's instructions and the portrayal of the anguish she experienced as she watched the two ascend the mountain. I watched as Isaac lay willingly bound to the altar and Abraham stood with the knife over his son, poised to obey, expecting God to either deliver or resurrect.

The second time she played the song, she invited the women to close their eyes and listen to the lyrics. The words of the chorus repeated over and over, "When you bound me, you found me. Now fear doesn't hold me. Hineni, Hineni." *Here I am*. Before she played the song the third and final time, she declared, "What you are seeking, you will find in the binding."

I had idols that needed to be bound to the altar, and they did not want to climb up there willingly. I was seeking a life of transparency, vulnerability, and authenticity. I was seeking women around whom I could be the fullest version of myself. I didn't want to be someone they admired or accepted because of my status or followers but simply because I was one of them: sharing the same language, understanding each other's pain, and walking in similarly uncomfortable cute shoes. To receive the belonging I desired, my idols had to be bound. The idols of self-preservation, control, and the pride of wanting to appear like I had it all together. All three needed to be bound for me to be free from the fear that held me. "Here I am, God." I cried as the room once again filled with the song: "Hineni, Hineni."

Since that evening, something changed in me. I'm a bolder, freer, more open version of myself. I am not afraid of being fully known. I see God in small details I used to miss. I behold Him beholding me—overseeing the activities of my days. The longer I gaze at Him, the freer I become. I've come to realize I am not everyone's cup of tea. I'm a little spicy like Chai tea. You may prefer Earl Grey or Lemon Zest. (All the tea is good.) I fit in the places where I belong. You fit in the places where you belong. They don't have to be the same places, though some will be. I found the fullest version of myself in the binding—in the surrender of my idols of self-preservation, pride, and control. Binding is not something we should run from but rather something we should run toward because in the "Here I am, God" we experience Him more deeply.

After the binding, you are the same person you were before, but the encounter takes you to a deeper level of comprehension about who you are apart from fear. Just as the binding of Jesus resulted in the full revelation of His identity, this binding leads you to a fuller revelation of who you are becoming. It's a process and there will be times you may have to return to the altar when fear returns or other idols arise. Remember that you become what you behold. As you behold the compassionate God who is slow to anger and abounding in steadfast love, you become a one-of-a-kind expression of the image of God on this earth.

Behold the Glory of God

Psalm 19:1 — "The heavens declare the glory of God; the skies proclaim the work of his hands."

Practical application — Behold the majesty of God's creation as a reflection of His glory. Take time to marvel at the beauty of nature. Spend moments contemplating the greatness of God revealed through His handiwork. From the people in your life and cherished pets you share space with to the trees and wildlife outside your home, allow the beauty of creation to inspire worship and praise. Gaze upon God's glory displayed in the world around you.

Exodus 33:18 — "Then Moses said, 'Now show me your glory.'"

Practical application — Like Moses, desire to behold the glory of God in your life. Prioritize intimacy and communion with Him. Ask Him to give you a longing to experience His presence in a deeper way. Come away for times of prayer and reflection. Ask God to reveal His glory to you. Open your heart to encounter Him in new ways. As His glory transforms your perspective, look again. Reexamine that problem. Look again at the prodigal child you've been praying for. Reevaluate your weakness. Behold His glory covering these situations and infusing them with hope.

Psalm 24:7–10 — "Lift up your heads, you gates; be lifted up, you ancient doors, that the King of glory may come in. Who is this King of glory? The LORD strong and mighty, the LORD mighty in battle. Lift up your heads, you gates; lift them up, you ancient doors, that the King of glory may come in. Who is he, this King of glory? The LORD Almighty—he is the King of glory."

Practical application — Behold the King of glory. Open the gates of your heart and welcome the Lord. See Him lifted high. Submit to His sovereignty, authority, and power. Seek to dwell in a life of perpetual worship. Allow the King of glory to reign over every aspect of your life. Surrender to His relentless love. Build your beliefs around the truth of His Word as you behold the Lord Almighty.

Daily Unveiling

1. What gift will you bring the King? What limitations are you attaching to the value of your gift?

2. Today is an opportunity for you to have a *hineni* moment. What do you need to bind to the altar?

3. A gift is only a gift when you release ownership. Pray this simple prayer: "God, all I have is Yours. Receive."

Visit www.davidccook.org/access or scan
this QR code with the camera on your
phone to watch Beholding Video No. 3.

Access code: known

Part II

BECOMING

Chapter 10

THE TENSION OF BECOMING

Somewhere between the hustle of life's demands and the lack of quiet moments for your soul, you may have lost something of great worth. Perhaps it has been lost for so long, you no longer recall possessing this treasure. Or perhaps you've simply lost the ability to recognize its value. This lost treasure is your identity.

People may have tried to tame it. Vision quenchers tried to extinguish it. Destiny thieves have been attacking it. But still, the fullness of your identity remains in the fabric of your being because inside of you resides an innate treasure that is unexplainable and unreproducible. Your identity is a paradox as unique as your fingerprints. It is both sensitive and strong, powerful and yielded, at peace and at war within you. This exquisite treasure confirms in your innermost being that your life has purpose—*you* have purpose. It provides the peace of knowing who you are amid the tension of the unknowns of life.

Parents become empty nesters. Wives become widows. Employees retire. The young age, titles change, and roles shift. We live in a world that is constantly changing. The tension of shifting seasons can leave you feeling like you are about to snap or it can pull you into the place of purpose and destiny. When life surprises you with change, it can be hard to determine if you are at a breaking point or at the point of breaking through into a deeper understanding of who you are. You may sense a divine invitation to something, but you do not know the details of the journey or even if it is one you dare embark upon.

This is the pressure of becoming. Much like a grain of sand turns into a pearl through pressure and aggravation, the process of becoming will not always be comfortable. The tension arises from the disparity between how you view yourself and how an infinite, all-knowing God sees you. It is an unraveling of the old that will set the stage for the new. Before we enter the wide-open spaces of grace to be fully who we are, there must be a dismantling of old identities, limiting beliefs, and constraining labels.

"What if there isn't one thing?"

This heart's cry was a turning point in my understanding of becoming and embracing my God-given identity. I sat in a wicker chair outside a small coffeehouse chatting with a friend. The temperature had already hit the nineties, making iced coffee the only reasonable option. With her iced white chocolate mocha in hand, my friend leaned back in her chair with a deep sigh. Her hot pink and orange kimono blew in the breeze as she laid bare her soul.

"Every coach I have ever worked with tells me I must determine the one thing God has placed me on this earth to do," she said. "But what if there isn't just one thing? What if there are multiple things? What if

I am passionate about one thing and yet also feel called to be a part of something else completely unrelated? How am I supposed to choose?"

Her question tore into my soul, reverberating inside of me. I, too, had believed the lie of "one thing." At the time of our coffee date, I had been working full-time for twenty years in clinical practice as a board-certified internal medicine physician. Since the age of five, all I ever wanted was to be a doctor. It was all I had ever known as a career, and it had become my identity.

Whether I was socializing in the foyer at my church, sitting in the stands at my son's basketball games, or pushing a cart through the aisles of the grocery store, I was acknowledged by all who knew me as "Doc." I do not think some of those who greeted me even knew my first name! Medicine was not only my career, it was the box others placed me in. Don't get me wrong—it was a box I enjoyed. I had well-defined roles within the box. I felt confident and secure. The box removed the need for me to grow in my knowledge of myself and God. But seasons change and failure to change with them can leave you wanting, empty, and depleted. When you find yourself in a box without the ability to grow, it becomes a tomb.

What boxes have you found yourself in? These boxes can be a title, career, position, hobby, or anything else that describes what you do but not who you are. What labels have been bestowed on you by others? Consider the ways people refer to you in conversation. Maybe you've been identified as "the pastor's wife" or "Joey's mom" or some other descriptor that places limits on your identity or is dependent on a specific season. These boxes can be comforting or necessary within a certain context. But when the season changes it can leave you feeling as if one or more boxes have been stripped away.

Maybe your kids are grown and flown. Perhaps you've made a job change. Maybe you've moved and find yourself in a community that has no idea about your "boxes." Sometimes the shifting is not external but internal. We change as God draws us to deeper levels of intimacy, trust, and surrender. Fear abates and courage breaks forth. Grief evolves into tenderheartedness toward fellow sufferers. Joy breaks forth out of our struggles. Peace rests upon our trials. Love settles our objections. At times a heart-healing, life-changing encounter with God ushers in a new season. Spaces where you once dwelled no longer have the capacity to contain the new thing God is doing in your life.

> When you find yourself in a box without the ability to grow, it becomes a tomb.

This is where the tension arises. In new seasons, our boxes no longer serve us. A label, career, title, role, or degree may outlive its usefulness. Consider the boxes you've enjoyed occupying. These roles or titles or descriptors may have made you feel comfortable, important, or known. There is no shame in the box. The confinement of the box, however, can lead to stagnation, unfulfillment, restlessness, and depression. The problem is not the box—it is our belief that we must choose only one.

What if there is not only one thing? That is the question I want you to consider. What if the tension you have been feeling is the pressure of staying in a box you have outgrown? What if this dissatisfaction is the holy stirring of a spirit that knows it has untapped treasures?

What if the restlessness is not a need to be filled but a need to uncover what has been buried inside?

Most of us are multi-passionate people with many goals and aspirations. Our minds are flooded with ideas, desires, and God-sized dreams. When we are told we must find the "one thing" that we were made for, we end up minimizing the rest. Let us look at how we can use the various passions and talents that God's given us in a way that does not leave us strained, drained, exhausted, and wanting to try to figure out the one thing. Let us exchange the "one thing" for the freedom to experience, enjoy, and explore all the avenues He has for us.

To do this, you must get comfortable with living out of the fullness of your identity. Just as there are many facets to your personality, your identity also possesses many variables. Our creative God has hidden treasures inside each earthen vessel. Most of us have only begun to scratch the surface of what God has deposited within us. Being fully known will push you past the labels—those that are self-imposed and the ones you've picked up along the way from others. You will have to surrender preconceived notions about yourself. You will have to be willing to transform how you articulate who you are.

I spend a lot of time mentoring and coaching women within my membership community. During our calls, I often ask, "What is God speaking to your heart? Where is He currently leading you?" I didn't expect for these questions to be difficult, but about 80 percent of women will hem and haw rather than answer them directly. They seemingly refuse to put a stake in the ground to declare: "This is what God is doing in my life."

I try to keep my cool, I really do, but sometimes the Alabama heat gets my blood boiling, and I cannot hold my tongue. During one coaching call with a group of ladies, I got so frustrated I exclaimed, "Why is it so hard to say what you feel God is speaking to you?" After a few uncomfortable moments of silence, a woman in one of the video squares raised her hand to reply. "I know God has called me to write," the middle-aged woman said timidly, "but I do not see myself as a writer. I am just ... me."

A moment of honesty has the power to change everything. In her transparency, she had opened the door to the area most in need of healing—her identity. The problem isn't that we cannot hear God or even that we do not know what He is calling us to do. The problem is we cannot see ourselves doing what He said because we do not see ourselves the way He does. This is where we must begin—pulling back the veil to confront the places where we refuse to believe what God has spoken and who we believe ourselves to be.

When you think about identity, what does that mean to you? I want you to go deeper in your understanding of this word. You likely have heard a sermon or read a devotional about your spiritual identity. You already have an idea of what the Word of God says about who you are: you are a child of God; you are fearfully and wonderfully made; you are a co-heir with Christ; you are seated in heavenly places; you are the redeemed of the Lord; you are His beloved; you are the bride of Christ; you are more than a conqueror.

These statements are an important starting point. The Bible is chock-full of wonderful truths about your spiritual identity. But I think too many of us have stopped with a head knowledge about who we are in Christ without allowing that truth to find wild, fearless expression in our lives! When we go beyond a biblical explanation of spiritual identity, we discover God also uses our natural identities to carry out His work in the world. Some of us are thinkers; some are feelers. Some love to talk, while others are quiet and observant. Some grew up in broken homes; some experienced the joy of healthy families. God can use each identity to accomplish His perfect will. What is your natural expression of God? Think about who God is calling you to be in the space, place, and time in which you have been chosen to abide.

This is the deeper part of us we do not always recognize. These inner workings can keep us on the fringe of freedom within our work, daily tasks, and creative endeavors. True freedom comes with the ability to be fully known without the fear of rejection or the shame of insecurity. It is an inner peace you feel when you are free from the need for approval because you know whose you are and what He has entrusted to you. To experience this peace, I must seek to understand not only my identity in Christ but also my unique natural identity.

Consider some of the ways the word *natural* is defined:

- being in accordance with or determined by nature
- growing without human care
- closely resembling an original: true to nature
- implanted or being as if implanted by nature: seemingly inborn

If you and I were attending a conference and the host asked everyone to stand up and introduce themselves, what would you say? What is your one-line description of yourself? Do you have your elevator pitch nailed down? Can you explain who you are in sixty seconds or less? I tried to do that for years. I produced a snappy statement to sum up my identity. But each time I rattled it off, something seemed wrong. Minutes after sharing, I would think, *But that's not all I am. Not even close.* I always felt like I was denying parts of myself to fit roles people already associated with me and felt comfortable seeing me in.

Unearthing new parts of your natural identity means stepping out of some of the boxes from your past seasons. This is not for the faint of heart. You must be willing to risk exposure. This journey of self-discovery calls you to deeper vulnerability and greater courage. It is an opportunity to see God's strength made perfect in your weakness as you draw a line in the sand and declare the end of some seasons so new seasons can flourish.

How has God been expanding your capacity to see yourself through His eyes? Where is He stretching your faith and showing you more about who you are? Do not resist the tension. Sit with it. Be still in it. Let it challenge you. Let it push past your doubts. Let it overcome the things holding you back. Let it breathe life into the dry and desolate places. Let it reveal to you new aspects of your God-given identity.

The work you are currently doing may not yet be the full expression of your natural identity. It could just be the level of expression you feel comfortable sharing with others right now. Some of your roles and pursuits are pit stops not destinations. This process of becoming will require experimentation as you find the courage to try new things. Each new opportunity is a chance for you to live out of your natural identity at the speed of your surrendered yes. That statement may sting a little. It stung when I first realized the biggest barrier to being at peace with my identity was me.

Pace Yourself

My journey began over twenty years ago. I was fresh out of medical school and getting acclimated to the thought of being an independent physician rather than a resident under someone else's authority. In my car, on my way to take my final board examinations, I experienced what some would call a vision. I was worshipping and listening to sermons to calm my nerves when, suddenly, I was no longer in my car staring at the road but on a stage staring at an auditorium full of women. I stood on the stage of a large arena with rows and rows of seats. I was petrified. I recall thinking, *Why am I on the stage?*

As I looked out over the sea of women, I watched them begin to dry up like raisins in front of me. The scene was terrifying. I opened my mouth in shock. It's not like I was about to speak; I had no words to say. But as my mouth opened, I saw the women restored to health. I was so stunned by what I saw that I closed my mouth. Again, the women started to shrivel.

Suddenly, the picture was gone and I was back in my car driving. This transpired in mere seconds. Despite its brevity, I have not forgotten the experience all these years later. It was a life-changing encounter that completely arrested me. After it was over, the force of my sobs shook me and forced me to pull to the side of the road. Not knowing what I had witnessed, I prayed it would never happen again. What I did not know at the time was that as I was beholding God, He was guiding me to becoming the woman He saw when He looked at me. God had given me a glimpse of a part of my natural identity that remained hidden to me. He knew it would take decades for me to accept my calling to speak. Thankfully, our natural identities do not have an expiration date.

Rest assured, if you've been resisting becoming who God's calling you to be, this is a no judgment zone. When I talk about failing to surrender our yeses, I speak from personal experience. For years after seeing myself on that stage, I refused to acknowledge what God had shown me. At the time it occurred, I was terrified of any type of activity that would expose me to criticism, judgment, or rejection. Public speaking was one of my worst fears. The thought of standing in front of even a small group of people was emotionally crippling. In grade school, I was the kid who would rather write a fifteen-hundred-word essay than give a five-minute talk to the class. You can imagine my alarm, when, after I had signed my first book contract, my publisher informed me I was expected to speak to groups about the book. *What? I did not see that in the contract!* Not one book would have been written had I read the small print.

But God is gracious and patient with us. He gently leads us at the pace of our yes. It started with agreeing to lead a small Bible study for couples in my home. My husband and I had no idea what we were doing, but we were desperate for connection in our new town so we said yes. (Sometimes it helps to have a partner in crime when you make that leap!) I still did not see myself as the woman on the stage. My living room was not an arena; my couch was not a stage. But one yes led to more yeses.

Even after years of speaking, I called myself a reluctant speaker and would say, "I feel God has shoved me into being a speaker." I said this because I could not yet identify with the person I was becoming. Communication is a part of my natural expression of God on the earth. He has placed this desire inside of me. But in my mind, I was a doctor. That is what I had studied for and spent years of my life doing.

There was not enough room for both callings—or so I thought. As a result, I spent many years stuck in the tension of becoming.

We have all heard stories of people who functioned in one capacity for many years and then, out of nowhere, they started doing something new. We try to make sense of these transitions by giving them names like midlife crises. But when you see these individuals functioning in their new field, they do not appear to be in crisis. In fact, they are often their happiest selves, filled with joy, purpose, and newfound boldness. This is what it looks like to function from your natural identity.

Maybe you have spent a lot of time and energy in a vocation or calling and yet you keep feeling pulled toward something you have never done. You may not have had a vision like I did. Perhaps it was a dream or just a "what if." Have you ever tried something you've never done before, and it felt strangely familiar? You were a "natural"? When new experiences feel like home, dig deeper. What was awakened in you that has been asleep? What was longing for release that has found expression? Those are moments when we step into our natural identity. And although you may not know that person yet, it is the person God already knows you are. Every time God takes you into a new place, think of it as a journey. It may feel stressful. That is the tension of becoming. As your understanding of who you are expands, you will feel the pulling, but it will enlarge your opportunities. When you are standing in those moments of capacity building, look for the places where peace remains, those moments where you are at peace with yourself.

That feeling comes when you are working from a place of rest. As you operate out of your authentic self, you will feel peace. You may not even recognize that part of your identity yet—a part that has been hidden or underutilized. But when you are grounded in the fullness of your natural identity, you will experience unexplainable peace and contentment, and emotional rest you did not know was possible.

Being fully known and stepping into your God-given identity is not something you do on your own. As you behold God and give Him your yes, He reveals these truths to you through your relationship with Him, your testimony, your abilities, and your spiritual gifts. As He makes Himself known through you as His unique child, those around you encounter Him in amazing ways. You become more truly yourself as you develop a deeper connection with His heart's desire for you.

I have had the privilege of standing with many women in the tension of becoming. This place is often marked by unknowns and can be messy. It shines with the glitter of what could be and is plagued by the bitter taste of past disappointment. You hear the tension when, in the wake of an amazing opportunity, a friend says, "That looks risky!" You experience it in your own negative self-talk: "Who do I think I am? I could never do that. What would people say?" As you step into the deep waters of your natural identity, you will experience opposition.

Whether you are twenty-five or seventy-five, it's time to embrace the tension of becoming, step more fully into your natural identity, and recover what has been lost. This book won't offer you a formula or easy steps to live a better life. In my experience, self-help books can leave me feeling even more imperfect, confused, and ill-equipped for the journey. My heart's desire in this "Part II: Becoming" section is that it would usher you into tension-breaking moments. I hope it challenges you and provides encounters with the One who can bridge the gap between the war in your mind and peace in your soul. The last thing any of us needs is more pressure. Now is a time for release. Release the fears. Release the doubt. Release the anger. Release the hope deferred. Release the grief. Release the trauma. Release the comfortable and the safe. Now is the time to throw away the boxes that have confined you and step into the wide-open space of being fully known.

Become a New Creation

Isaiah 43:18–19 — "Forget the former things; do not dwell on the past. See, I am doing a new thing! Now it springs up; do you not perceive it? I am making a way in the wilderness and streams in the wasteland."

Practical application — Instead of dwelling on past failures, become a person who notices the new thing God is doing in your life. Behold His ability to make a way where there seems to be no way and to bring beauty out of brokenness. Be open to the leading of the Holy Spirit as He provides new ideas, opportunities, and relationships. Be willing to be surprised by God. Step out in faith to experience new blessings as He opens doors.

2 Corinthians 5:17 — "Therefore, if anyone is in Christ, the new creation has come: The old has gone, the new is here!"

Practical application — Becoming new in Christ involves a continual process of growth, renewal, and restoration. Grow in wisdom with God. Discard your old ways of thinking and behaving by the renewal of your mind. Allow Him to restore your curiosity and love of adventure. Reflect the character of God by living a life marked by righteousness and holiness. Align your actions and attitudes to mirror God's heart to become an agent of His love and grace.

1 Peter 1:23 — "For you have been born again, not of perishable seed, but of imperishable, through the living and enduring word of God."

Practical application — Becoming a new creation in Christ involves the implantation of the seed of the Word of God. You become rooted and grounded in the truth of Scripture, allowing it to shape your desires and orchestrate your actions. As a result, your life bears the fruit of spiritual rebirth, producing love, joy, peace, patience, kindness, goodness, faithfulness, gentleness, and self-control.

Daily Unveiling

1. Reflect on the difference between your spiritual identity and your natural identity.
2. What fears war against you expressing more of your natural identity?
3. Remain in the tension of becoming. Pray this simple prayer: "God, stretch the boundaries of my understanding of who You've made me to be."

Chapter 11

BECOMING
UNRESTRICTED

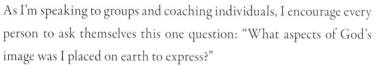

As I'm speaking to groups and coaching individuals, I encourage every person to ask themselves this one question: "What aspects of God's image was I placed on earth to express?"

If we are created in the image of God, then there are facets of His character and goodness uniquely and intentionally placed inside of us to express within our families and friend groups, in our homes and workplaces, and in our communities.

Whenever our family visits a new place, we love touring the city by way of a scavenger hunt. An app asks questions and provides clues that encourage us to explore the city. With each answered question, we learn more. Nothing has been hidden from us; we are just unfamiliar with the area. We do not know what is available in this new locale, so we need a little prompting to help us explore all that's available to us. This is what it looks like to walk with God and discover the unique ways we reflect Him.

God told Abraham, "Go from your country, your people and your father's household to the land I will show you" (Gen. 12:1). In essence, you and I are called to go on a scavenger hunt with God! The land God wants to show each of us is the territory He has given us. The lives we are to impact. The kindness we are to give. The hope we are to impart. The joy we are to bring. The love we are to share. It is unfamiliar territory, and we need guidance to fully explore it.

Unfortunately, we will likely run into barriers that stand in our path, impeding progress and preventing further exploration. They are like invisible fire walls that we run into headfirst. A fire wall is a fire-resistant barrier used to prevent the spread of fire. Typically, fire walls divide a building into separate sections so that a fire in one area won't burn down the whole structure.

Hardwired into our design is a longing to experience the unbridled presence of God—a consuming fire that ignites our spirits and transforms our lives. Yet, in our pursuit of more of God in our lives, we often construct barriers, like fire walls, in an attempt to confine the flames within the bounds of our comfort zones. As we delve into understanding these fire walls—physical, emotional, spiritual, and relational—we uncover the subtle ways they inhibit the flow of God's fiery presence in our lives and limit the depth of our encounters with Him.

Physical Fire Walls

Imagine your body as a sacred vessel, a temple where the divine meets the natural. In our fast-paced lives, we often neglect this sacred space, treating our bodies as mere vessels for surviving this life rather than a sacred sanctuary for spiritual communion. Despite our souls crying for rest, we push ourselves past exhaustion. Our bodies become a battleground, bearing the scars of neglect, abuse, and overexertion. But regardless of the condition of our weary frames, we are bursting with potential for renewal and restoration. The flames of God's presence can burn brightly once more.

> Imagine your body as a sacred vessel, a temple where the divine meets the natural. In our fast-paced lives, we often neglect this sacred space, treating our bodies as mere vessels for surviving this life rather than a sacred sanctuary for spiritual communion.

Picture yourself surrounded by nature's beauty, the gentle caress of a breeze, the warmth of the sun on your skin—reminders of the Creator's intimate presence in every fiber of your being. Through practices of self-care—restful sleep, nourishing meals, mindful movement—we can honor our bodies and invite God's healing.

Emotional Fire Walls

Close your eyes and take a journey into the depths of your heart— a landscape marked by valleys of pain, mountains of fear, and rivers of tears. Here, amidst the wreckage of broken dreams and shattered hopes, you build walls of self-protection, shielding yourself from the vulnerability of authentic connection. But it is in your brokenness that you will find the greatest beauty, for within your cracks lie the capacity for healing, growth. Through these cracks, the flames of God's love will illuminate and warm even the darkest corners of your soul.

Imagine the freedom of letting go—the weight of shame lifting from your shoulders, the chains of fear falling away—as you surrender your heart and give yourself permission to feel all the feelings. Through practices such as journaling, counseling and therapy, and participating in authentic community, we discover inner strength to overcome emotional challenges and create space for God's presence to melt away our fears and awaken us to the fullness of life's possibilities.

Spiritual Fire Walls

Somewhere between the mysteries of God and the complexities of theology and doctrine, we attempt to define the undefinable. We erect rigid beliefs about who God is and who He is not. And yet there is so much we do not know, an endless expanse of God's omnipotence and omniscience. Instead of only attempting to stand in His presence, imagine the thrill of free-falling into the net of His grace. How exhilarating would it be to abandon your own agenda and trust in the infinite wisdom of an all-knowing God. Through practices of spiritual exploration—praying, reading Scripture, worshipping, serving, and fellowshipping—we break down spiritual fire walls, allowing God's power to reign over every aspect of our being and illuminate our path.

Relational Fire Walls

Imagine yourself surrounded by a circle of like-minded individuals—all united in love, empathy, and mutual support. Instead of erecting walls of judgment, we build bridges of compassion and connection. In vulnerability, we find community. Vulnerability is like a beacon that draws in your people. Shared laughter and communal tears usher in the warmth of companionship and the comfort of knowing you are not the only one. Through practices of relational restoration such as transparency, forgiveness, and reconciliation, we allow the light of God's love to shine through our relationships.

Becoming unrestricted is the process of being free from the mindsets, patterns, and beliefs holding you back. Part of breaking free is tearing down the fire walls that keep God's presence within the narrow confines of our protected zones and relegated to our own limiting ways of thinking. Instead, we should be like a child running down the stairs on Christmas Day, overflowing with anticipation. Think of each new breakthrough as an exhilarating discovery along the route of your scavenger hunt. By knocking down your physical, emotional, spiritual, and relational fire walls, you open yourself to the unquenchable fire of God to ignite within you a passion to release what's inside—your portion of heaven to be shared on earth.

Unpack Your Passions

"Sometimes you don't know what makes you happy," my friend said. "You just know what doesn't." I nodded and remained silent.

"There's a big contrast between the way I feel when I'm doing my main job and when I'm engaging in other activities," she continued, pacing back and forth along the length of her kitchen counter. "I am so happy and alive doing these other things. It's becoming more obvious that my current job is not fulfilling me, but I worry about making a change. What will people think of me? How will I pay my bills? I'm sure people would think I'm flaky if I launched this new thing that I really want to do, but I also wonder if God is disappointed in me for not having the faith to fully follow Him and just do it!"

Maybe like my friend you find yourself confined to a job or position that brings you no joy. You're not alone. Admitting that you're not satisfied takes courage, especially when you find fulfillment in other areas of your life. The contrast between the joy you feel when you are engaging authentically and the monotony of your day-to-day work responsibilities can be disheartening. Noticing this discrepancy, however, is the first step toward making a change and finding what resonates with your natural identity in your current season.

You may hesitate to act because you worry you will look foolish to others. And in your hesitancy, you feel you may have disappointed God who you see as expecting big things from you. This can be the hardest qualm to overcome. If you grew up in a strict religious setting or have experienced being hurt by the church, you may view God as mean and overbearing. This is the reason we begin by beholding His character and seeking to truly understand how He views us. Rightly viewing who He is gives you the confidence to become the person He has created you to be. He is faithful to love you through the becoming.

When you find yourself in this position of wanting to explore the unconventional, you will feel fear and uncertainty. This is a normal part of the process. If you've built your identity around a certain profession or title, you may worry about departing from it. God may call you to something completely different from anything you are currently doing. He does not consult your list of acceptable options. No, He shreds your list and provides you with possibilities that make you take a step back, drop your mouth open, and proclaim, "Say what now, God? You want me to do *what*?"

Keep in mind that true satisfaction does not ask how much money it can make in three months or what type of return on investment is possible. The only guarantee with taking this road less traveled is that there will be joy. You will experience the contentment of living with purpose as you impact others and grow in intimacy with God. Don't fall for the world's lie that says, "Once you find your passion, it will never feel like work." It will probably still feel like work. You will have responsibilities, challenges, stretching moments, successes, and failures. But you will experience the joyful satisfaction of being fully known.

Uncovering your passions is not vocational fairy dust. You can't sprinkle on passion and call it a day on the job. Knowing what you are excited about and what brings satisfaction helps you to identify where God has graced you with the power to start, endure, and remain. Passion produces a rhythm of work that is refreshing, restorative, and restful. It pulls from the reservoir of your emotional, mental, physical, and creative energy reserves while simultaneously pouring into your spiritual reserves. As you pour out, you get filled up. In the outpouring, you are restored.

Think about your current job or set of responsibilities and examine your limiting beliefs. Have you felt God speaking to you about changes in your current situation? He is gracious and kind. He may choose to go at a pace you're comfortable with or He may nudge you into the next thing. If you are resistant to taking big strides, He will patiently guide you forward. If you are yielded and trusting, strap in for the ride of your life. Sometimes the speed of the process may correlate with your tolerance to the uncomfortable and willingness to step into the unknown. Ask for faith to trust the Holy Spirit with a pace you can only manage with Him.

Becoming unrestricted often comes with a sense of urgency to act on what God has awakened inside you. As we gain a deeper understanding of God's heart and are moved by the things that move Him, we will desire to do more. However, in some cases, there may be a prolonged period of being before doing. The vision of what God is doing can come long before it is fully realized.

Joseph, whose story is told in the book of Genesis, had dreams of his future leadership success. Annoyed by his bragging, his brothers threw him into a pit and sold him into slavery. He spent years being faithful in unfavorable conditions before stepping into a position of leadership. Another example is David, who was anointed king but didn't take the throne for many years, enduring humbling jobs like playing music for the king and long nights sleeping on damp cave floors. Over a decade elapsed between the apostle Paul's conversion and his first missionary journey. Several of those years were spent in an Arabian desert being instructed by God.

Vision and calling often come in embryo form. We might receive a glimpse of a life to come that requires a long germination period. A premature birth is not God's desire. He doesn't set you up to fail. Instead, He gives you time to develop the necessary character, fortitude, support systems, and knowledge to sustain the vision He has for you. We may get impatient in the germination stage. We are confident He has shown us something, but when months and years pass without further evidence, we grow weary and doubt what He revealed. It takes so long to see any evidence of what we saw that we abort. Relinquish the timing, process, and outcome to God. Trust that He is helping you become the exact person you need to be to carry the vision to full term.

Become Available to God

Psalm 119:105 — "Your word is a lamp for my feet, a light on my path."

Practical application — By anchoring your life in the truth of God's Word, you become available to receive His guidance and direction. Just as a lamp illuminates the path ahead, God's Word provides clarity and wisdom for your journey. This involves regularly studying and meditating on Scripture, allowing its principles to shape your decisions and actions. As we become people of the Word, we are equipped to walk in obedience to God's will, becoming effective instruments in His hands for His glory.

1 Samuel 3:10 — "The LORD came and stood there, calling as at the other times, 'Samuel! Samuel!' Then Samuel said, 'Speak, for your servant is listening.'"

Practical application — Like Samuel, when we adopt a posture of listening to God, we become available to hear His voice. By cultivating a heart attentive to God's leading, we position ourselves to respond when He calls. Make room in your schedule for time alone with God and be receptive to His prompting in your life. As you become an attentive listener, you will find God communicating with you regularly throughout the day.

Acts 20:24 — "However, I consider my life worth nothing to me; my only aim is to finish the race and complete the task the Lord Jesus has given me—the task of testifying to the good news of God's grace."

Practical application — When we prioritize the mission that God has given us, we become available to fulfill His purposes with single-minded devotion. Like Paul, our primary goal becomes advancing God's kingdom and proclaiming the gospel. However, you must be willing to cast aside your own agenda and preferences to pursue God's mission wholeheartedly. As we become fully committed to following Him, our lives become a testimony to His grace and power at work within us. When we faithfully steward the opportunities and resources God has given us, we become available for greater responsibilities in His kingdom.

Daily Unveiling

1. How do you define the value found in both being and doing?

2. Often, the Holy Spirit will lead you at the pace of your obedience. What is your pace?

3. Is there a vision God has shown you in embryonic form? Would you like one? Ask Him. Pray this simple prayer: "God, show me what You see in me."

Chapter 12

BECOMING
UNRESTRAINED

If you're nerdy and you know it, clap your hands. *Clap! Clap!* Yep, I'm clapping ridiculously over here. I love science and research—which is why there are stacks of books all over my house! My dog, Rosey, is a tiny Havanese weighing less than ten pounds. I fear for her safety when she gets too close to one of my stacks of books. I start imagining the old cartoons where the character gets flattened by a heavy object and turns into an accordion.

My latest book purchase was a journaling study Bible with wide margins for doodling and notes. When I spend time beholding God in His Word, I become inspired. New songs spring to my mind, and I like having a place to jot down lyrics right in my Bible. The first time this happened I thought, *Oh, that's cute. I wrote a song.* Then people who heard the little tunes I'd sing as I walked around started to comment on them, causing me to stop and ponder what was happening.

I was awakening to a talent I did not know God could use for His glory. I had always been Saundra the doctor; never Saundra the songwriter! But my casual praise to the Lord became an outward expression of heaven on earth. Eventually, I had a collection of my songs recorded and produced. I was elated and started thinking about what dress I would wear to receive my Dove Award. I'm only kind of joking; I had high hopes for where my album might take me. Many told me how my lyrics blessed them, but that's where it ended. No shiny trophy or public recognition at the end of it all.

The recording was a great gift to share with family and friends. It offered a level of transparency I had rarely disclosed. One evening I was visiting my in-laws. After dinner had ended, the plates had been cleared, and everyone was trying to digest the massive quantity of food consumed, the family gathered around to make some music. This was not uncommon. My husband's family is musical and traveled together as a singing group during his childhood.

I settled in to listen as I had done many times before. But the first bar of music had me on my feet. They were playing one of my songs! They had learned their parts by ear, and my niece was singing my lyrics in her clear, strong voice. It was a beautiful moment of connection, and I felt honored.

Later that evening, I played the recorded version of that song again and I noticed something. The disappointment I felt in its lack of success was gone. I had judged the reception of my music based on one metric—a Dove Award. God had judged it based on my willingness to become unrestrained—to release what was within me, to invest my talent, and trust Him for the return on my investment. What I received that night was more valuable than any award I could have received.

Being Multitalented

In the parable of the talents (Matt. 25:14–30), Jesus describes a master who entrusts his servants with a varying number of talents based on each one's ability. To one, he gave five talents; to another, two; and to another, one. The master goes on a journey, and while he is gone, the servant with five talents trades with them and earns five more. The servant with two talents likewise doubles his investment. But the servant with one talent freezes in fear and hides it in the ground.

When the master returns, he celebrates the first two servants because they have multiplied what he gave them. But he rebukes the servant who did nothing with his one talent. He calls him wicked and lazy. He then casts this servant into outer darkness. Through this parable, Jesus illustrates how God has uniquely gifted each of us and expects us to multiply those gifts for His purposes and glory.

In the parable, a talent is a unit of money. However, the concept of investing our abilities and skills, also known as talents, fits the story Jesus was telling. Many of us think of ourselves as having only one primary talent. While you may have a specialty, God has placed a wealth of resources and abilities within you. The lessons you have learned, the trials you have overcome, the problems you have solved, the relationships you've built, the victories you've won—all of these are housed in the vault of your life. It is your very own Fort Knox full of treasure you've accumulated through life experiences. You are also likely skilled at more than one thing. Maybe you are great with Excel spreadsheets at work, and you're an amazing home decorator in your spare time. In becoming unrestrained, the goal is to pull out some of the talents you may have been hiding away and begin to use them.

Many of us fear embracing our multitalented identity would be prideful or scatter us in too many directions, leaving us overwhelmed and exhausted. So we shrink back from fully expressing the multiple facets of our God-given identities. We limit ourselves to one acceptable career, ministry, or mission while neglecting the other talents He meant for us to multiply. We play it small, burying our talents in the ground out of fear or insecurity.

What if God has called you to be a "five-talent person"—one who invests multiple talents in His kingdom? Becoming unrestrained requires a close examination of the reason you may feel uncomfortable and unworthy of your multifaceted identity. Here are a few potential reasons.

You don't want to appear prideful. You may fear that expressing multiple talents will come across as self-promotion. You want to have an acceptable amount of talent or power (more on people-pleasing later). In the parable Jesus told, the servants had no say over the number of talents they received. The amount was the master's choice based on what he knew about each servant. Your competencies are not a work of your own doing (1 Cor. 4:7). Recognizing, honoring, and using what God has placed in you is not prideful when the glory goes to Him.

You feel confused about how to use your gifts. When you discover you have multiple passions and gifts, it can be unclear how they all fit together. You may struggle to understand your core message or mission, flip-flopping from month to month. Don't beat yourself up over not having it all figured out. As you faithfully steward the talents the Master has given you, God will guide your steps and bring clarity to your path. Each talent does not need to link to the others. They can exist independently to be used for His purposes in whatever measure and sphere He decides.

You compare yourself with others. When we see others who seem to have a clearly defined singular calling, we may feel flaky or less spiritual. Keep in mind that God has not called you to someone else's path. He has laid out a unique road for each person. One servant received five talents while another only received one. Each servant was equally valued by the Master and each had the opportunity to hear the words, "Well done." Whether you've been given one burning passion or multiple outlets through which you can reflect His image, use what He's given you! As you become familiar with your talents, you will see the personal nature of God as He leads you on your own path.

You practice false humility. Maybe you don't want to appear to think too highly of yourself or make others feel less than, so you downplay the gifts deposited in you. False humility does not bring glory to God and limits your ability to be a blessing to those who need the gift you're hiding away. True humility is agreeing with God about who He says He is and who He says we are. It's not self-deprecation or self-criticism but accurate self-assessment based on your time spent beholding Him and the truth of His Word. When you view Him as worthy, you need not fear expressing the talents He's given you.

You struggle with people-pleasing. Fearing what others will think if you branch outside of your expected roles and core competencies is another stumbling block. As you make choices based on the approval of others, insecurity may cause you to bury the very talents God desires to multiply. His opinion of us matters far more than the voices and opinions of people. He is the One we must honor and obey.

When you are a multitalented person with a multifaceted identity trying to fit into a single-calling existence, you will end up frustrated, discontent, and unsatisfied. No matter how successful you have become at your "one thing," the hidden passions and talents inside will give you no peace until they find a place of expression. Your responsibility is to faithfully invest your talents as He leads and leave the outcome to Him. When it comes to the multiplication, assume a kneeling posture. Whether you feel you've received little or much, cast it all before the throne. Give yourself permission to explore each possibility the Master has placed within you.

> His opinion of us matters far more than the voices and opinions of people. He is the One we must honor and obey.

What Talents?

Each person's set of talents and gifts will look different. Here are some questions to help you start identifying your talents and passions and to see how God has uniquely equipped you to express Him.

1. What activities come easily to you that seem difficult for others? Often, our talents feel so natural to us that we assume they are no big deal, but they are clues to how God has gifted us.

2. What do you find yourself drawn to instruct, fix, or improve? When you see a problem that needs fixing, and you feel compelled to help or support, pay attention. There is likely a talent lingering there.

3. What makes you smile ridiculously? What do you do that causes you to lose track of time because the joy of doing it causes you to feel alive? This feeling is a signpost pointing you in the direction of a talent.

4. What moves you to tears? The things that break your heart are often tied to a God-given passion that can lead you toward an investment opportunity for your talent. Let your holy discontent lead you to your calling.

5. What causes you to feel righteous indignation? Is there an injustice that fires you up or an evil you feel compelled to combat? Righteous anger may indicate an anointing to use your abilities to help right that wrong.

As you reflect on your answers, resist the urge to explain them away. Don't diminish the talents you identify just because they come easily to you. View them as avenues to explore. For example, having a heart for orphans doesn't negate your ability to lead worship. You could do both. Perhaps not at the same time but within different seasons of your life as God directs. The key is to allow all your talents and passions to converge in you being fully known.

Once you have identified your talents, allow God to use them to produce a return for the kingdom. Look for opportunities to use your talents. Practice putting yourself out there in small ways. As you are faithful with little, God will entrust you with more. As you get the hang of it, begin taking risks. Experiment with different outlets where you can express your talents. As you try new things, you will gain greater clarity on how God wants to use you. Focus on cultivating Christlike character that will sustain the calling. Humility, integrity, and honor will help you nurture your talents in a way that glorifies God and blesses others. Make spiritual renewal a priority as your influence grows.

Remember that through your individual talents and passions you carry precious cargo that will advance God's kingdom on earth. Stop limiting yourself to "one thing." Lean into your God-given potential. Resist comparing yourself to others or feeling you must bury parts of your identity to fit in.

Take hold of the truth that God has fashioned you to become what you behold. You don't have to strive in your own strength. You need only to surrender your talents back to the One who gave them to you and follow where He leads you to invest them. When you start investing your gifts and taking risks for His kingdom, you step into collaboration with the Lord where anything is possible.

Follow where He leads you to shine His light into the darkness. Then watch how He will multiply and bless your efforts as only He can. That is the adventure of becoming unrestrained. Embrace your natural identity, express your multiple talents, welcome each sacred calling, and prepare to be amazed at what He can do through you.

Becoming Light

Isaiah 60:1–3 — "Arise, shine, for your light has come, and the glory of the LORD rises upon you. See, darkness covers the earth and thick darkness is over the peoples, but the LORD rises upon you and his glory appears over you. Nations will come to your light, and kings to the brightness of your dawn."

Practical application — As you receive God's light, His glory becomes increasingly evident in your life. Arise and shine, allowing His glory to radiate through you into your home, workplace, church, and community. Brighten the path for those around you, inviting them to encounter the life-changing power of God's radiant presence.

John 8:12 — "When Jesus spoke again to the people, he said, 'I am the light of the world. Whoever follows me will never walk in darkness, but will have the light of life.'"

Practical application — To become a light-bearer, you must align yourself with the truth and righteousness of Christ. Jesus illuminates the path of all who follow Him. As we meditate on Jesus' saying, "I am the light of the world," we are reminded of our calling to become like Him, reflecting His light in the darkness. It is a continual process of abiding in Him and allowing His light to shine through every aspect of our beings.

Luke 11:33 — "No one lights a lamp and puts it in a place where it will be hidden, or under a bowl. Instead they put it on its stand, so that those who come in may see the light."

Practical application — Becoming light is a deliberate choice to shine rather than hide. You must accept the price of visibility and the potential to be misunderstood, judged, and rejected. Remember that the rewards of staying small and hidden pale in comparison to the joy and freedom of being unrestrained. Position yourself to shine with the light of Christ for all to see. In doing so, you invite others to come out of their own darkness and into God's light. You have a responsibility to reflect God's glory through your character, attitudes, and actions. In standing out, you become a vessel through which God's glory shines, drawing others to praise Him.

Daily Unveiling

1. Answer the five questions in the "What Talents?" section.

2. What are some of the reasons you hesitate to share these talents with others?

3. Talents are not to be hoarded but invested. Pray this simple prayer: "God, use my talents for Your glory."

Chapter 13

BECOMING UNDAUNTED

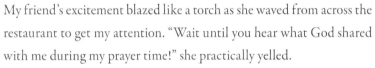

My friend's excitement blazed like a torch as she waved from across the restaurant to get my attention. "Wait until you hear what God shared with me during my prayer time!" she practically yelled.

My friend Andrea was not her usual self. Instead of being quiet and reserved, she was nearly jumping out of her skin! Her abrupt change of disposition alerted me to the fact that something significant had happened. The woman embracing me was vibrating with enthusiasm.

As someone who prefers calm conversations over a latte or hot tea, I typically recoil from hyper people. This version of my friend was new, and I was not a fan. I had met Andrea during a time in her life when she was walking through some difficult challenges. Those strained and stressed years had quieted her, dampening her energy and joy. The Andrea I knew wore pastel colors. From her hairstyle to her toenail polish, nothing was flashy or overbearing. Everything about her was subtle. When we spent time together, she did not provoke me to any type of emotion, good or bad. She was a comforting presence ... until now.

As I approached the table, she was nearly screeching with excitement. Her hair was in a messy bun. She wore a bright, floral tank top and her sandaled feet showcased electric blue–polished toenails. When I had walked into the sandwich shop to meet her for lunch, her back had been to me. I'd taken one look at the colorful shirt and wild hair and didn't recognize her. I moved on to search for an empty booth to wait for Andrea to arrive. It took me a second to realize this exuberant woman waving at me *was* Andrea!

Everything about the moment felt off, and my friend quickly noticed my uneasiness.

"What's up?" she asked.

"Maybe I should be asking you that question," I said judgmentally. I had the feeling we were on the verge of a fight, but I couldn't for the life of me figure out why. Why was I irritated by my friend's excitement? What about her change of personality was triggering this reaction from me?

"I don't know what's wrong with me," I said, softening. "It must be my hormones." Forcing a smile, I continued, "Please, share what God showed you."

That was all the permission Andrea needed. Her words gushed out like water from a broken dam. She told me about her vision to create a place of respite for single women in need of a fresh adventure with God. Her kids were all young adults living their lives. They visited as they were able, but since her recent divorce, she had found herself spending more and more time by herself. Her husband's betrayal had wounded her deeply, and that damage required years to heal. She was finally at a point where she could believe her past pain could be used by God, and this was what had her so excited.

She continued to share: "I didn't want to get too worked up until I could figure out how it would all come together. But I think I've found the location I want to purchase, and it's near the coast in France!"

I almost choked on my appetizer. "How did you find a property in France?"

She explained the backstory of a friend knowing a friend and so on. By now my mind was tuning out everything she was saying. All I could think about was the many reasons this was a horrible idea. I was glad my friend wasn't acting depressed and defeated anymore, but I didn't feel like she needed to turn her life upside down and move thousands of miles away either.

The moment she paused to take a breath, I shared my concern. "Andrea, I love your vision, but I don't think moving to France is a good idea."

We locked eyes across the table. I was ready to stand my ground and fight for what I believed was best for my friend. I was not about to sit back and let her make a crazy, life-ruining decision. My position was gently upended by six words.

With a patient smile, she replied, "I wasn't asking for your permission."

I wish I could say I had my big girl pants on that day, but I did not. I was more like a toddler in a dirty diaper. I was fuming mad, and I didn't care who knew it. A part of me wanted to grab my friend and shake some sense into her. Before I could move, she moved first. She extended her hand across the table, palm up. Our eyes locked again. Hers conveyed a message I could not interpret. *Compassion? Understanding? Love?* I put my hand in hers.

"Your friendship has been a healing balm in my life these past five years," she said. "You've cheered me on when I was at my lowest points. You've loved me when I was my least lovable. I get it. I don't want this to change either. I don't want to lose the routines we have built, but this is my next step with God. My mind is made up. I don't need your permission, but I would love to have your support."

From that day forward, our friendship moved to a new level of intimacy and depth. Girl time changed from in-person to virtual. Her breakfast time was my dinner time. Connecting became more complicated, but we made it work. I watched my friend evolve into a woman who was undaunted by external storms. Circumstances no longer intimidated her. Neither did challenges—and there were many. Once she had settled a matter in her heart between her and the Lord, she was not moved by the words or opinions of others.

Andrea is living fully known. She navigated the heartbreak of betrayal by beholding God's comfort and grace. She allowed what she saw in Him to change her. I watched her become a new creation—ready and available to be used by Him. She now uses the talents God has given her in an area of ministry she feels called to. It is a place of belonging. She has purchased multiple properties across France where women from around the world can come to start fresh following a major life setback.

Looking back on how I first responded to her vision led me into a time of self-reflection, and I didn't like what I saw. A major part of my resistance had nothing to do with how the move to France would affect Andrea's life but how it would affect mine. Like Andrea, you, too, may encounter people in your life who will resist you entering into being fully known.

Under Friendly Fire

Before you get to the point where you want to reveal what God's shown you to others, you've likely already walked through the battlefield of your mind. You've had to overcome the internal dialogue of insecurity and doubt. You've had to choose following God's plan over reclining in your comfort zone. Upon conquering those giants, you hope you will be met with cheering fans who are a hundred percent on board with what God is doing. Many times, this is not the case. Instead, you may find yourself on a new battlefield. The first battle was a lonely quest of introspection that you had to maneuver on your own. The next one will spill over into your connections and commitments, touching your relationships and what others expect of you. This encounter will include the people who know you best.

Have you shared your dream or vision with someone, only to have them shoot it down like I did with Andrea? They may say, "Are you sure you heard from God?" or "Do you have enough experience to do that?" They may inquire, "Where are you going to find the money?" or say, "Have you thought this through? I don't think it will work." Statements like these are like bullets of discouragement straight to your heart. They are especially painful when they come from people you didn't think would oppose you.

This "friendly fire" could come from your spouse, best friend, parent, or anyone whose opinion and approval you value. You know they love you and you anticipate they will be just as happy as you are about your new venture. Then, when you open up and they push back, you feel disappointed and defeated. The battle of overcoming your own misgivings may have left you weary and exhausted, setting you up for greater disappointment when others don't support you. At that point, the choice is yours: continue forward or be swayed by their negative input.

I'm not suggesting you should be careless or ignore valuable insight and information. Scripture tells us to seek godly counsel. But I fear when we come under friendly fire, we are too quick to relinquish God-sized visions. When the people we love, and who we know love us, refute what we've heard God saying, it can cause us to second-guess ourselves. We care about their opinions and may be blinded to their hidden agendas.

If you had told me I had a hidden agenda with my friend Andrea, I would have been offended. I love my friend and want what is best for her. And yet there was an underlying reason even I could not identify that caused me to attack her vision. I wanted her near. I didn't want things to change between us. I was at peace in our relationship and did not want the disruption of something new. My inner motive was a desire for stability. This agenda wasn't malicious, but it could have become a vision blocker if my friend had not courageously held her ground. The thing about hidden agendas is that they can be concealed from both parties. That is why it's important to dive a little deeper into this topic, so you can identify an attack of friendly fire and know how to respond.

As you expand beyond your comfort zone and explore the depths of your potential with God at your side, you will inevitably encounter resistance, including from those you love and hold dear. Don't be surprised when you come under friendly fire from the people who know you best. Try not to be offended. Your shift also shifts things for them. It's likely that they do not realize that they may be operating from fears that have nothing to do with you.

To become the person God is calling you to be, you must navigate pushback with grace and wisdom. You must have grace for the person offering resistance, recognizing it often stems from a place of fear and uncertainty. And you must have discernment to accept true wisdom and discard the rest. There are times when their input is for your benefit and comes from a pure place. Evaluate each concern with God to determine if what you are encountering is wise counsel or a hidden agenda. There are four types of friendly fire people may use to attack you as you learn to be undaunted by outside resistance.

1. The Loss Attack. As you explore life beyond your normal routines and patterns, you may encounter the "loss attack." In this confrontation, a person is apprehensive due to potential losses associated with change. They may worry about how your shift will disrupt their comfort or happiness. They may fear losing the security of a cherished relationship or the comfort of deeply held beliefs being overturned by your new perspective. An example is a mother who doesn't want her grown child to move away because she fears not being a part of his life or seeing her grandchildren. Approach these concerns with empathy, understanding there is a fear of the unknown and even grief feeding the person's reservations. Respond with gentleness, emphasizing your confidence in God and faith over fear. Engage opposition with compassion, seeking to maintain a healthy relationship where you feel free to move as God directs.

2. The Safety Attack. A person may initiate this type of confrontation out of concern for your well-being. He or she may point out the perceived dangers of what you are proposing. These individuals will caution you against taking risks and warn you of potential pitfalls. They will urge you to stay within the safety of what is known and secure. An example of this would be a family member who urges you to keep your unsatisfying job rather than embark on a riskier but more fulfilling career. While their primary motive may be protecting you, it's also possible their advice comes from their own anxieties about venturing into uncharted territory.

God calls us to trust in His plan for our lives, even when it involves risks and unknowns. You can balance the tension between safety and growth by considering their advice and remaining steadfast in your convictions. You can honor your own aspirations and the feedback of those who care about your safety.

3. The Defeat Attack. In this friendly fire attack, we encounter those who view every challenge as an insurmountable obstacle. They seem intent on telling us all the reasons our idea is destined to fail. Through their pessimism, they undermine our belief that all things are possible with God. Their relentless pessimism can be disheartening. They will dismiss your aspirations and magnify the flaws they see in your plan. They may truly love you, but their defeatist mindset arises from their own insecurities, doubts, and limitations.

I've regularly encountered this type of attack on my path of becoming, and it takes a toll on the spirit. However, strength and support can be found within a positive and uplifting community. I once had a friend tell me that I probably couldn't get a book published because the market was saturated with material like mine. I'm thankful that I was in an encouraging writers' group who urged me to press on.

4. The Intimidation Attack. This type of pushback employs tactics of control and coercion, as the individual seeks to hinder your progress by wielding power over essential resources such as finances or provisions. This is the least friendly of the attacks and is a type of opposition you should be on the lookout for. An example would be a father who refuses to pay for college unless his child goes to the university of his choice. Those launching this form of attack may use their influence in your life to instill fear about a lack of supplies, knowledge, or ability. It can feel as if they are using their authority or influence to bully you into submission. This type of psychological manipulation stems from a desire to maintain a sense of control. By standing firm and seeking support from trusted allies, you can resist intimidation tactics and continue pursuing your goals with courage and conviction, trusting in God's provision and guidance.

Moments of Hesitation

Remaining undaunted by fear and the opinions of others requires courage and intentionality. Too often, I have found myself dwelling in moments of hesitation even when I am sure I've heard clearly from God. I shrink back to shield myself from risk, but I end up feeling restrained. When I hesitate to act in obedience, it hinders me from authentically expressing my gifts and experiencing the joy that comes with releasing them.

What if we dared to abandon ourselves to the beauty of the present moment and fully express ourselves without reservation? What if we dared to step beyond the boundaries of fear and uncertainty, trusting in the greater glory that lies ahead?

> When the path ahead seems
> fraught with unknowns, take
> comfort in the knowledge that an
> all-knowing God goes with you.

The longer I behold the love, power, and sovereignty of God, the more I am convinced that true safety lies in Him. He is our sure thing amid a world full of uncertainty. Obedience to God comes with divine protection, even if you're stepping onto a path you never imagined He'd ask you to travel. The path may appear daunting, darkened by valleys of hardship and mountains that seem impossible to scale. When the path ahead seems fraught with unknowns, take comfort in the knowledge that an all-knowing God goes with you. Be aware of His closeness and behold Him. Watch how He moves.

Yield to His guidance. Follow the path of obedience as far as you can, trusting He will provide new instructions when the time comes. Venturing into the unknown with unwavering confidence in God is a daily walk of faith and exercise in trust.

In moments of hesitation, I've learned to lean into the gentle whisper of God's voice, guiding me forward and reassuring me with grace. Rather than allowing fear to hold me back, I've chosen to embrace the moment as an opportunity to become more trusting, more thankful, and more aware of His presence. It's a process of surrendering myself to the joy of obedience. In becoming undaunted, I've found freedom in knowing I'm pleasing God and gratitude for the nearness of the Holy Spirit.

Become Free

John 8:36 — "So if the Son sets you free, you will be free indeed."

Practical application — Embracing the freedom offered by Jesus Christ leads to a transformation of our identity and purpose. By accepting Christ as our Savior and Lord, we become liberated from the power of sin and death, experiencing true freedom in Him. This involves surrendering our lives completely to Jesus, allowing Him to reign supreme in every area of our lives. As we walk in the freedom that Christ provides, we become individuals who are empowered to live boldly for His glory, fulfilling the purpose for which we were created.

Galatians 5:13 — "You, my brothers and sisters, were called to be free. But do not use your freedom to indulge the flesh; rather, serve one another humbly in love."

Practical application — Becoming free is not a license to indulge in your own desires, but an opportunity to serve others in love. You become liberated from selfishness and self-centeredness. This involves adopting a mindset of humility and servanthood, and seeking to use your freedom to bless and uplift those around you. As you live out your freedom in Christ by serving others, you become one who reflects His love and compassion to a world in need.

2 Corinthians 3:17 — "Now the Lord is the Spirit, and where the Spirit of the Lord is, there is freedom."

Practical application — Surrendering to the leadership of the Holy Spirit leads to a life of freedom. By allowing the Spirit of the Lord to direct your path, you become liberated from self-reliance and pride. Allow Him to empower you to live according to God's purposes. As you walk in step with the Spirit, you become free to live out the fullness of your identity, experiencing His peace and presence in all your coming and going.

Daily Unveiling

1. Who are your friendly attackers? What might be their hidden agenda?

2. Choose to give them grace. How can you ease their fears and bring peace back into the relationship? Do you need to set boundaries with certain people?

3. Though the vision may take time to mature, wait on it. Pray this simple prayer: "God, strengthen my resolve to remain faithful."

Chapter 14

BECOMING UNSHAKABLE

"God is not disappointed in you. He has promoted you. You are in a set-apart season."

My spiritual mentor's words washed over my heart like a soothing balm. They dispelled the whispers of inadequacy haunting my thoughts. The weight of this assurance covered me like a blanket and ignited a flicker of hope in my soul. In that moment, the room seemed to glisten with possibility. Memories flooded my mind. Times I'd felt overlooked. Talents I'd brushed aside like forgotten treasures. Gifts I'd left unopened. Opportunities I'd left untouched. I found solace in the reassurance of the woman's words—God sees. He promotes. He sets apart. These words went deep into my soul, awakening dormant seeds to the promise that winter would soon end, and spring was coming. In that hallowed exchange, I dared to believe God was not done with me yet.

There have been years when I have sensed I've been in a set-apart season. This period often came with the loneliness of no one understanding my discontentment and the isolation of feeling like an outcast. If you think you're in a similar place, you may feel like God has forgotten you or you have fallen off His radar. During this time, there is a pulling away happening, but it is not God withdrawing from you. More likely, it's the pulling away of your unstable beliefs and flawed truth as they are uncovered. Perhaps you believed you were successful in your career because of your dedicated prayer life. But when you lose your job, you are forced to reevaluate your beliefs.

While it may feel as if God has abandoned you, it's quite the opposite! This is a time when He pulls you into the secret place to prepare your heart for what's ahead. The need to be heard is replaced by the need to hear God more clearly. By His grace, you lay down your expectations and surrender to His plan. Your desire to understand *why* is placed on the altar and consumed by the fire of understanding *who* God is in your life. *Why* bows low to *Who*, which is on the throne. Questions are hushed in the face of pure obedience based on your relationship with a God who can be trusted. Obedience prompts you to yield your whole heart, including its assumptions, preferences, and expectations. Hope deferred loses its power to make your heart sick because you have given God full power to choose on your behalf. Your hope is in God and God alone.

The Set-Apart Season

Do you feel hidden? You recognize your talents, but they seemingly go unnoticed by others. You carry a God-sized dream that appears impossible to obtain. Times with no friends coming around may make you feel isolated. The days are long and lonely, but you are not alone. This appointed time-out is not a punishment. It's a time of promotion in your intimacy and identity, which will impact your influence. This time serves a purpose to help you become unshakable and is a critical step toward being fully known.

Something happens to you during a set-apart season. It is an inner work invisible to those on the outside. Inside, a deep chasm opens. You start to notice the changes between how you have always been and who you are becoming. You are the same person but not the same. This phase doesn't make you a different or better version of yourself. Instead, it welcomes all of you to come forth. The red carpet is rolled out and everything inside of you is invited to join the party—the creative, the contemplative, the analyzer, the leader, the encourager, the teacher, the supporter, the giver, the lover. It is the season when you must choose if you will answer the one-word invitation Jesus gave to His disciples: *Come.*

The Lord invites you to come know Him in His fullness. To know yourself in the fullness of the amazing and distinct ways in which He created you. To know the ways you fit perfectly into God's plans. To know the joy of living openly. To recognize and experience the power of the Holy Spirit at work in you, through you, and around you. To come behold, become, and belong.

The set-apart season prepares you for the hard stuff. It fortifies you against the darts of bitterness, self-pity, ridicule, and humiliation aimed at you. It quickens your spirit to hold fast to truth. It trains your hands to release anything that would slow you down and hinder your progress. You are in a holy training ground.

Let's look at some ways you can recognize this phase in your life. One indication is becoming aware of your talents and your courage rising. You look for opportunities to be stretched outside of your comfort zone. But in this season, the opportunities don't come. You may feel overlooked, even when you are qualified or perhaps even overqualified. You will have to fight against envy and jealousy as you see others get the opportunities you desire. The set-apart season trains you to celebrate what God is doing in the lives of others. Can you be thankful and praise God when the blessing you desire goes to someone else? Can you see their victory as a kingdom win? Can you put aside selfish ambition for a greater glory?

During this time, you may experience persecution for your faith or stance for the gospel. Character attacks, wrongful accusations, misjudgments, or mistreatment from others can be common occurrences. Under such pressure, it is crucial to trust God's guidance regarding when and how to respond. James 3:8 warns us "No human being can tame the tongue. It is a restless evil, full of deadly poison." The tongue requires holy training. In the set-apart season, you learn how to discern when to speak and when to be silent along with how to respond when others are spewing evil at you. This is training on how to speak life and not death in every situation.

> The set-apart season trains you to celebrate what God is doing in the lives of others. Can you be thankful and praise God when the blessing you desire goes to someone else?

There will also be internal battles concerning your identity. Who you are becoming on the inside doesn't align with your current circumstances. This discrepancy leads to feelings of frustration and self-doubt. Remember, this is temporary and not a forever situation. It does not define you, nor is it an indication of wrongdoing. It's part of God's process. There are numerous examples of set-apart seasons throughout Scripture. My favorite is the life of King David. Years before he could claim the throne, he endured a set-apart season of being hidden and overlooked.

In Psalm 13, David laments his struggle with the tension between his present reality and the destiny he knows he was meant to fulfill. Read his words slowly and let them sink in.

> How long, LORD? Will you forget me forever?
>   How long will you hide your face from me?
> How long must I wrestle with my thoughts
>   and day after day have sorrow in my heart?
> How long will my enemy triumph over me?
> Look on me and answer, LORD my God.
> Give light to my eyes, or I will sleep in death,
>   and my enemy will say, "I have overcome him,"
>   and my foes will rejoice when I fall.
> But I trust in your unfailing love;
>   my heart rejoices in your salvation.
> I will sing the LORD's praise,
>   for he has been good to me.

In the set-apart season, you may feel disheartened, forgotten, left out, and unwanted. However, this is the training ground for belonging. You are being stripped of the weight of fitting in and earning the approval of others. You learn to appreciate the art of "being" without accolades and recognition for what you do. The goal is to value and desire most the applause of the Holy One over all others. You discover there is room for contentment without public acknowledgment. God often uses this time to address our hunger for adulation and to teach us that He is the one worthy of all praise.

The Lord does not allow this time in order to break you down. He allows it to give you a breakthrough. Recognize these periods of growth as a prelude to the blessings in store. Your coming-forth season might be right around the corner. God uses the set-apart season to prepare you for the greater responsibilities of what He's promoting you to. He may be preparing you to serve others in a greater capacity. He may be planning to entrust you with a greater level of influence and authority. This promotion may be an increase in the level of provision He trusts you to steward or the grace He pours out on everything your hands touch.

During your set-apart season, it will feel like everything is being shaken. No part of your life is off limits. Every unstable thing within you is brought to the surface so that you may become unshakable. It's a developmental process of building a strong foundation of God-aligned values, relational integrity, and mental resilience. These qualities will serve you well when your time to emerge on the scene arrives.

Remember to trust in God's plan, stay committed to your dreams, and allow this time to develop your skills and character. Keep trusting hard, stay focused, and believe God knows what He is doing. Embrace this period as a necessary part of becoming and have faith the best is yet to come.

Find What Fits You

As you navigate your set-apart season, you will encounter well-meaning individuals who will offer you their formulas for success. While they may have valuable wisdom to share, resist being pulled into self-help models or cookie-cutter methodologies of achieving the things you long for. In your desire for reinvention, only God offers you real transformation. Stand firm in your trust in God and His perfect timing. He has a unique strategic plan just for you. What works for someone else may not be the right fit for you. Resist running to broken cisterns that hold no water instead of running to the spring of living water (Jer. 2:13). Always filter advice through the lens of Scripture and prayer, asking the Holy Spirit for discernment.

I was once encouraged by a business coach to withhold my best content to create false scarcity to drive sales. This method was not what I saw reflected in Scripture. As someone who is living with the mind of Christ, I knew I was called to operate from a place of abundance and not lack (John 10:10). I was becoming one who could be scandalously generous out of the overflow of what God had given me. I could trust Him to replenish me as I used what was in my heart and hands. Giving fits me, not scarcity and fear. I knew I could focus on serving well and meeting needs and let Him handle the rest.

In your departure from your set-apart season, there will be giants to overcome—fear, insecurity, and impostor syndrome are a few common ones. Don't be surprised by these giants; you have already been prepared to take them down. This past season was not in vain. It restructured you and you are stronger for it. Just be sure to use what fits you and stay true to what you know. Remember the story of David suiting up for battle against Goliath? King Saul tried to give him his own armor, but it didn't fit. David wisely decided to step onto the battlefield with what he knew would work—a slingshot, a few stones, and a whole lot of trust in God.

You have history with God. There are victories under your belt. Though the current giant may look and sound different from the ones in the past, you know what fits and what works for you. Don't try to force yourself into someone else's armor. Just because everyone else is starting a podcast doesn't mean you should. Broadcasting may not be a part of your armor. Photography may be what fits you. Lean into the talents, passions, and resources God has provided, even if they seem small or insignificant. Surrender all you have to Him and watch what He does through your faithfulness with a little. That's where His power flows—at the intersection of your mustard-seed faith and His great ability.

Another key to building well is discerning the specific arenas God has called you to. Not every opportunity is the right opportunity. Not every audience is your assignment. Yes, someone needs to serve in children's church, but is it you? Is that the arena where you fit best? Ask the Lord for wisdom on where to invest your time and energy. When you operate in your God-assigned arenas, that's when you'll find His favor and open doors.

When you are working from a place of praise and gratitude using your talents, it becomes worship. Your love for what He loves burns away selfish ambition and a craving for the approval of people. Set fire to your own agenda and watch Him resurrect something beautiful from the ashes. On a practical level, this could mean a total overhaul of your current vision, goal, or priorities. If it becomes apparent that something you desire isn't aligned with God's plan, be willing to let it go, even if it's all you've ever known or wanted. Trust Him to give you fresh manna that reflects His heart and advances His purposes.

As you fix your eyes on Him, you will find the stability you need to stay the course. You'll find it easier to trust God's timing and provision. You will hold fast even when progress is slow, and change seems far off. The process may feel risky, but in the long run it will pay off as you experience the joyful satisfaction of donning well-fitting armor in the arenas God has prepared for you. He is building an unshakable kingdom on the earth, and you enter into it as you become unshakable.

Become a Worshipper

Psalm 95:6–7a — "Come, let us bow down in worship, let us kneel before the LORD our Maker; for he is our God and we are the people of his pasture, the flock under his care."

Practical application — Embracing the call to worship leads to a transformation of our relationship with God. As you become a worshipper, you cultivate a heart of reverence and adoration toward Him. This involves setting aside time to draw near to God in praise and appreciation. In your going low, you raise Him high in your soul and spirit. In the kneeling, you flex your intimacy muscle and heighten your awareness of how awesome He is.

John 4:23–24 — "Yet a time is coming and has now come when the true worshipers will worship the Father in the Spirit and in truth, for they are the kind of worshipers the Father seeks. God is spirit, and his worshipers must worship in the Spirit and in truth."

Practical application — Becoming true worshippers involves living a lifestyle of praise and gratitude to the Lord. Rather than being relegated to a few songs on Sunday morning, you develop a worship mindset and a daily practice of thankfulness. Instead of only singing with the praise team on Sunday mornings, you cultivate a heart that sings when no music is playing. Your worship reflects the truth of what you know about God's love, grace, and mercy. The Spirit of God within you communes with Father and Son. All three receive when you worship in Spirit and in truth. This is the fragrance of true worship, and it is a scent heaven can't resist drawing near to enjoy.

Psalm 100:2 — "Worship the LORD with gladness; come before him with joyful songs."

Practical application — Become one with an attitude of worship. Engage in your activities with gladness and joy. Instead of approaching your work or activities as an obligation or burden, view them as a privilege and delight. Let everything you do be something you are privileged to do because of your talents and not something you are forced to do. Cultivate a spirit of gratefulness in your worship, rejoicing in God's goodness. As you come before Him with an uplifted disposition, let a new song burst forth from within you. Approach worship with a deep sense of awe, allowing God's presence to captivate your heart and mind. As you behold the splendor of His holiness during worship, you become a reflection of His glory, magnifying His majesty and greatness.

Daily Unveiling

1. What is your armor? What tools have worked well for you?

2. In which arenas have you already found favor? Where is your gift welcomed (not just expected)?

3. Worship is an act of beholding and becoming. Pray this simple prayer: "God, as I worship, transform me."

Chapter 15

BECOMING UNSTOPPABLE

Whether you realize it or not, daily you are becoming. You are learning to recognize your God-given talents. You are becoming a new creature never before seen—the fully known version of you. You are becoming a generous, passionately free you. You are becoming bolder, more courageous, and more adventurous. You are becoming unstoppable. You will move when God says to move. Go where He says to go. Speak what He prompts you to speak. Serve as He leads you to serve. Now you need to figure out how not to burn out in this place of being fully known and fully available to God.

This was Sarah's predicament. Sarah was a forty-year-old multitalented woman who expressed her creativity in both her 9-to-5 corporate office job and her side hustle—an art studio. A single mother, she split her time between work and caring for her children. She embodied a woman doing all the things—paying the bills, living her passion, and raising a family, all while attempting to care for herself. Between the meetings and the milestones, Sarah was desperate for rest. She wanted time to stop so she could breathe and reconnect with the peace and joy that had somehow vanished from her life.

Can you relate to Sarah? Work is a blessing when it is done in alignment with God's purposes and precepts. But work without rest leads to resentment. You feel bitter about the time spent doing and the resignation of joy. To stay effective and enthusiastic and unstoppable, you need a rest strategy. Psalm 46:10 is one of the pillars of resting well. "Be still, and know that I am God." This verse is a divine rest strategy I have been implementing in every aspect of my life over the past five years.

When traveling to speak at churches or conferences, people will ask me, with a look of admiration, "How do you do it all?" Let me assure you there is nothing to gawk at here. I'm as flawed as the next busy woman. I war with rest. It goes against my nature. My heart is that of a longtime workaholic until I behold Him. Then I see the truth. I see that I am nothing apart from Him. I am empty without His presence and His Spirit. I am a branch in need of the true Vine.

Being asked, "How do you do it all?" led me down a path of mentoring and coaching women who also find themselves at the intersection of the sacred and secular. God has called them to influence a variety of spaces through the expression of their natural identities. They carry a deep reverence for the kingdom of God and possess the ability to share spiritual truths with those who do not yet know God in a way they can receive. With one hand stretched to heaven and one hand stretched to earth, they are vessels used by God to be repairers of the breach.

The stance of expressing one's God-given identity, even in the face of resistance, can take a toll on the body, mind, and spirit. During a time when I felt pulled in every direction, God brought me back to meditate on Psalm 46:10. Out of that experience, I developed my Abide-Act Framework. This framework provides a structured approach to working from a place of rest. As you apply it to your life, you will learn how to incorporate rhythms of rest in your weeks, gain clarity on your goals, and take Spirit-led action throughout the year.

The Abide-Act Framework allows you to craft your year with intention, breaking the twelve months into five ten-week blocks with an additional two-week sabbatical, or "bonus rest," period. These five blocks allow you to focus on specific priorities as the Holy Spirit leads so you can structure your year in a way that honors the Lord. Some of the exhaustion and lack of joy we experience is because we stay in seasons longer than God desires. Let your priorities be fluid and quick to shift with God. Having five opportunities throughout the year for God to clarify your direction helps you stay on His desired path for you, creating a sense of flexibility and flow.

One of the beautiful things about the Abide-Act Framework is how it empowers multitalented individuals to embrace the fullness of their gifts and callings. When you have many passions and interests, focusing on any one thing without feeling like you're neglecting the others can be challenging. This framework invites you to lean into the unique ways God has designed you, while still providing a structure for focused pursuit of your goals. By dedicating each ten-week block to a particular area of talent or calling, you give yourself permission to go deep in that direction for a season, trusting that your other gifts will have their time to shine in the future. This approach frees you from the pressure to do everything at once, while still honoring the multifaceted nature of your identity and purpose.

Each ten-week block could look completely different as He shows you where to put your attention and focus. By dividing the year in this way, you give yourself permission to flow with the Spirit's leading with dedicated time and energy to concentrate on the areas that matter most in each season. This framework recognizes that your priorities can shift and provides a flexible structure to lean into those changes. It accommodates both those who work full-time and those who are retired. The time spent engaging in Abide-Act activities each week is your call. You may flow freely in and out of times of resting and working, being and doing.

Multitalented individuals are often skilled at setting goals, but falter in the execution of them. Most of us have started a project that we never finished. We are excellent starters and poor finishers. With multiple passions and opportunities vying for your attention, discerning how to make steady progress toward your goals can be a challenge. The Abide-Act Framework emphasizes the importance of implementation, so that you finish what you start. Has your hesitation in following God fully been based on your lack of confidence in your ability to complete what you set out to do? Give yourself grace. Your lack of completion likely is not a reflection on your ability. It could be more telling of your flawed processes. Yes, you should begin with the end in mind, but you also need to work through the building blocks to set yourself up to accomplish the goal you initially set.

The Abide-Act Framework is a rest-centered way of cooperating with God. It bridges the gap between being and doing. It moves you from vision to execution by giving you specific time to identify the smaller action steps, or "building blocks," that will move you toward completion of your larger goal. By breaking it down, what once felt overwhelming becomes achievable.

The Abide-Act Framework

ABIDE Weeks 1–2: Two weeks of intentional rest.
ACT   Weeks 3–10: Eight weeks of purpose-focused work.

Each ten-week block follows a two-eight rhythm—two weeks of abiding followed by eight weeks of acting on the instructions received. In the abiding phase, you focus on connecting with God. Behold Him. Spend time enjoying His presence. Inquire of the Holy Spirit and seek clarity on what God would have you focus on over the next eight weeks. Don't do the work; seek His heart about the reason for the work. Why is the goal important to Him?

For years I had been asking God for community, yearning for deeper connections with others. I was disappointed I could not seem to find the type of group I was seeking. As I sat in His presence during one of my abide weeks, I felt the Lord's encouragement to create the group. The following two weeks, many friends who knew nothing about my plans shared their own need for greater community. Abiding gave me clarity and vision.

During the next eight weeks—the act phase—you will focus on doing the work to accomplish the goal. I like to further break down the act portion into two four-week periods. The first four weeks are all about strategy. This is where you will identify the building blocks needed to complete the goal. What are the smaller pieces of the goal that you will need to do first? It requires you to strategize, organize, and plan to see what is needed to cross the finish line. During the last four weeks, you arrange all the building blocks to complete the goal. These weeks are all about implementation and pursuing your goals with intention and consistency.

The group I felt led to create was no different. The eight-week act phase was needed to plan and implement. The process included naming the group, determining the core mission, setting a schedule, and deciding on a membership pricing structure. This project was not one that could be completed in ten weeks. It required multiple ten-week cycles with each cycle focusing on completing one of the above activities. I was still working full-time and only had a few hours each week to dedicate to the Abide-Act Framework, but with each cycle I got closer to completing what I started. A year later, Titus 2 Collaborative was born.

Sometimes a goal or vision will be massive, requiring multiple Abide-Act cycles that span perhaps years. Be flexible. You may discover that within a big vision, you will have a few ten-week cycles dedicated to goals that are not work-related goals such as mental, physical, or emotional renewal. God may halt outward progress toward a goal if there is a faulty belief or character issue in need of realignment. The Abide-Act Framework allows for this, as the achievement of the goal is determined by God and not you.

As I was building Titus 2 Collaborative, I spent one of my ten-week cycles solely on spiritual renewal. That extended abide phase helped me to see that I was struggling with fear of rejection. No one wants to start a group and have no one join. Rather than follow the instructions God had given me, my fear encouraged me to avoid the humiliation of failure. The action phase during those ten weeks was not to build the community but to build up my confidence and faith. Eight weeks of prayer, fasting, self-reflection, and conversation with spiritual mentors were the building blocks needed to fortify the foundation of my spirit.

This two-eight rhythm ensures that you are taking regular pauses to recenter in God's presence and gain insight before moving into action. Drawing from the New Testament story of Mary and Martha (Luke 10:38–42), this framework incorporates our need for both Mary and Martha qualities, times of stillness at the Lord's feet and times of service. Instead of getting caught up in unsatisfying busyness and ritualistic activity, you can move at the pace of peace with a God-centric plan. By structuring regular abide periods into your doing, you create space to bring your plans before God and discern what deserves your focus in each season. The framework helps you discover that sometimes what feels most urgent or exciting in the moment may not be the top priority from an eternal perspective. Those two weeks of abiding give you an opportunity to slow down, pray, and realign your agenda with God's plan. This concept is reflected in the words of Proverbs 16:9: "In their hearts humans plan their course, but the LORD establishes their steps."

The Abide-Act Framework provides a way for you to lean into your different callings in different seasons and avoid burnout. As you focus on one area during a ten-week span, trust that God will guide you in how to steward your other talents and interests in His perfect timing.

Maybe God will call you to learn a new skill during one block of weeks and prepare you to go on a mission trip during another. What makes this framework so exciting is its adaptability. Like cross-training at the gym, it allows you to flex new muscles and build greater strength in existing ones.

As someone with a strong work ethic and deep desire to be used by God, I have been prone to take on too much work. I have fallen into the trap of thinking my worth is tied to my productivity. I have believed that saying "no" is ungodly. The Abide-Act Framework lovingly challenges these assumptions, reminding me that my value comes from my identity as His beloved and not from the things I accomplish. By structuring regular periods of abiding into your year, you create space to discern which priorities are truly yours to pursue in each season. You learn to resist the temptation to overcommit, recognizing that sometimes the most productive thing you can do is to pause, pray, and look for the steps God has lovingly ordered for you to take.

Let's consider a practical example. During your two weeks of abide time, you feel God calling you to mentor college-aged women. As you seek Him during the first two weeks, God gives you His heart for these young women. You feel what He feels about them and love them as He does. Your goal might be to provide these women with biblical truths to encourage them to honor God with their sexuality by following His commands about purity in Scripture. Where do you begin? The goal might seem like too great a task. Most God-sized visions are too big for you; hence the term "God-sized." They will require you to depend on Him to complete the good work He is doing through you.

Following the two-week abide phase, the next eight weeks are dedicated to action. You might use the first four action weeks arranging the building blocks that will help you accomplish your goal. During this time, you think through the details, anticipate potential obstacles, and create a plan. By investing time and energy in this foundational work, you set yourself up to take focused, confident action in the weeks to come. This is where you transform the vision into an actionable blueprint. If ministry to college-aged women is your goal, this would be the time you spend exploring the best format, scouting a location, networking with others in similar ministries, choosing resources, and getting the word out.

The final four weeks of the Abide-Act Framework are the implementation phase. Using the blueprint you've developed, you set your initiative in motion. Whether your goal was to launch a new business, build a better relationship with a family member, host an event, take on a thirty-day fitness challenge, or get your message out to a new audience, it's time to courageously take a step of faith and trust God with the results.

In my example goal of ministry to college students, this is when you would begin mentoring, teaching, or influencing. As you dig in and do the work you've prepared for, you get to witness the fruit of your faithfulness and experience the joy of co-creating with God. Consider the following detailed example of what the ten weeks might look like for someone desiring to mentor college-aged women.

Week 1 (Abide): You spend time in prayer and fasting as you seek God. This is a time to slow down, listen for the whispers of the Holy Spirit, and allow God to fine-tune your focus.

Week 2 (Abide): The Holy Spirit highlights your passion for young women, particularly those who are college-aged. You are moved with compassion for them and desire to be used by God to serve them with your talents.

Week 3 (Act): Now you begin a planning phase to translate your vision into reality. This is where the rubber meets the road in terms of implementation. This week's building block could be fleshing out the vision God has given you. You feel called to start a relational mentoring group with the young women in your church community where you meet weekly.

Week 4 (Act): You aren't sure of the ideal time for such a group, so the next step is to reach out to five young women you would like to mentor to get their feedback.

Week 5 (Act): This week builds on the last as you evaluate the women's feedback on the best times to meet, their felt needs, and the topics they are interested in discussing.

Week 6 (Act): Now you have laid a foundation on which to move forward with intentionality. You set the first meeting two weeks out, choose your first topic, and invite the young women to meet at your home.

Week 7 (Act): You study in preparation for your first meeting and research icebreaker ideas.

Week 8 (Act): You prepare to receive the young women into your home by purchasing snacks and drinks. You reach out to each young woman, reminding her of the meeting and telling her you're excited to see her.

Week 9 (Act): You conduct your first meeting with the college-aged women.

Week 10 (Act): You celebrate completing this task. Regardless of whether two or five showed up, you are a finisher. You acted on what you received during your abide time. Reflect on the feedback you received from the young women. Take both your praise and your petitions into your next time of abiding for further instructions.

At the end of this ten-week cycle, you can reflect on what you have accomplished and celebrate the progress you've made. You've sought the Lord for His direction and taken Spirit-led action; now you witness the fruits. Then it is time to begin your next ten-week block, trusting God to illuminate your next area of focus during your abide time. During your next abide period, the instruction may be to continue your work with college-aged women, providing more clarity or guidance on how to serve them. Your next eight weeks of action could include developing a curriculum for mentoring or a plan for expansion. Enter each ten-week cycle open to hear how God will lead. Sometimes He has you continue what you are doing. Sometimes He will instruct you to pivot to something different for a season. Each time you pause to inquire ensures you will never get too far off track from His perfect will. The Abide-Act Framework creates a powerful strategy for accomplishing meaningful goals in partnership with God.

While dedicated focus is a key component of the framework, it also recognizes the importance of building in times of rest and realignment. Stay open to these rhythms of work and rest. Honor the fact that you are a whole person with needs and priorities beyond doing and achieving. You can be still and know you are known by God. The Abide-Act Framework is designed to help you step into your calling in a sustainable way. You will not be driven to burnout, but driven to the throne room, a place where you will be able to elevate God above all other desires.

As you break free from cycles of burnout and into cycles of reproducible grace, with the Holy Spirit's help, you become unstoppable.

The Abide-Act Framework is all about empowering you to be not just a dreamer, but a doer—someone who partners with God to translate the vision into reality. This structure invites you to confront what stops you from completing the things you start. It takes you on a journey of committed obedience, even when the request is unfamiliar or uncomfortable. You open yourself up to receive fresh insight and intelligence for the new things God is inviting you into. You recognize and say goodbye to seasons that have run their course.

This method is a life-altering tool for anyone who wants to live with greater intentionality. It helps you move beyond goal-setting to making and executing a plan. This allows you to experience the joyful satisfaction of a job well done multiple times throughout the year. As you break free from cycles of burnout and into cycles of reproducible grace, with the Holy Spirit's help, you become unstoppable.

As you use this method, don't be surprised if God invites you to release certain roles, identities, or strategies that you've previously clung to. Becoming requires a willingness to let go of what is familiar and comfortable to step into the new things God is birthing in and through you. This process of gentle surrender can feel vulnerable and disorienting, but it is often a necessary part of your journey to freedom and fruitfulness. By consistently returning to a place of abiding and listening for God's voice, you receive the courage and clarity needed to keep saying "yes" to His invitation to be fully known.

Become a Giver

Acts 20:35 — "In everything I did, I showed you that by this kind of hard work we must help the weak, remembering the words the Lord Jesus himself said: 'It is more blessed to give than to receive.'"

Practical application — In becoming givers, we cultivate a spirit of generosity and concern for those in need. This involves actively seeking out opportunities to extend a helping hand, whether through financial support, acts of service, or the blessing of encouragement. As you make it a priority to be sensitive to the needs of others, you experience the joyful satisfaction of filling others from your overflow.

2 Corinthians 9:7 — "Each of you should give what you have decided in your heart to give, not reluctantly or under compulsion, for God loves a cheerful giver."

Practical application — Becoming a cheerful giver shapes your attitude toward contributing. Rather than giving out of obligation or duty, you give willingly, motivated by love and gratitude for God's blessings in your life. This is a deliberate decision to steward your resources with an open hand, glorifying God through your trust in His abundance.

Proverbs 11:25 — "A generous person will prosper; whoever refreshes others will be refreshed."

Practical application — By becoming generous, you expand your giving beyond the physical. Give financially but also give in other ways, such as extending kindness, offering grace, and showing hospitality. As you refresh others with your generosity, you will also be refreshed by experiencing the satisfaction of making a positive difference in the lives of others.

Daily Unveiling

1. Reflect on John 15:4: "Abide in Me, and I in you. As the branch cannot bear fruit of itself, unless

it abides in the vine, neither can you, unless you abide in Me" (NKJV).

2. Based on this verse, how would you define the word *abide*?

3. In our connection to the true Vine, we become fully known. Pray this simple prayer: "God, help me to stay connected to You."

Visit www.davidccook.org/access or scan
this QR code with the camera on your
phone to watch Beholding Video No. 4.

Access code: known

Part III

BELONGING

Chapter 16

UNLIMITED GOOD

When we think about the various gifts, talents, and abilities God has placed within us, I like to think of an inanimate object in nature—for example, an oak tree. Reflecting on the tree's intrinsic capabilities helps me more fully visualize and understand how God has created me. An oak tree rises from the ground and can stand over one hundred feet tall with its branches lifted high. During its fruitful season, its leaves spread wide providing shade to anyone who seeks a reprieve from the heat of the day.

This is not the oak tree's only role. Like us, it has many purposes. While offering shade, the tree also serves as a place for birds to build their homes. It drops acorns to feed wildlife depending on it for nourishment. It pulls in and stores carbon dioxide and releases oxygen back into the environment. The oak tree is endowed by God with the ability to be a comforter, supporter, sustainer, and provider. Each role taps into one unique aspect of its total makeup and each role reflects God.

During the winter, after the leaves have changed colors and fallen to the ground, this tree looks barren and without purpose. But this time of barrenness is a purposeful reset. Even in that depleted, pared-down state, it still has many gifts to offer. The only difference is the gifts are the sacrificial yielding to the One who knows its days. The tree stops being fruitful because God says so. It doesn't resist pulling back from productivity. It does not cease being a mighty oak because of its need to rest.

Throughout its life cycle, it retains its full identity as an oak tree. It can be chopped into kindling to create a fire that warms your entire home. It can be cut, milled, and used in construction or flooring. It can be carved into a keepsake or cut into a rocking chair. From seed and germination to decline and decay, it experiences the goodness of God in all the seasons of its existence.

Preparation for the Seed

Numerous times in my life, I have been convinced that I was ready for whatever door God wanted to open next. It's exciting to get to a place in your walk with God where you are open to accepting a God-sized vision. You've pushed past your fears, stepped out of your comfort zone, and seized the day with a roaring, "Let's go, God!"

You may have a dream about starting a ministry or launching a business. Or perhaps you feel inspired to pursue an area of your gifting that you've never explored before. The excitement of the seed—the idea God has planted in your heart—can propel you into action before the soil of your soul has been adequately prepared to receive the watering of God's power. The best ideas are useless without the Lord of the harvest empowering them. An idea is a seed, and each type of seed has specific conditions needed for it to flourish and grow.

Allowing God to prepare you for planting sets you up to bear fruit in His perfect timing. It's an intentional decrease to prepare for the increase. It creates the setting for unprecedented growth. During those moments of early excitement, I often find myself running ahead of God's timetable. Who needs a timetable? "Not I!" said the woman running fast into overwhelm, exhaustion, and burnout. Acting as fuel, my enthusiasm catapults me right out of being and into doing. Dozens of half-finished projects started this way litter the ground in my rearview mirror. They remind me of past failed ideas and cause me to doubt if I'm good soil that God can use.

My friend Daniel has a homestead out in the plains of the Midwest. He lives off the land with very few provisions from outside sources. I have always viewed his way of living as difficult. I had never spent a day in his shoes, but looking in from the outside, I couldn't imagine homesteading for the things I need rather than just ordering them online. One day as we were sharing about our day-to-day lives, Daniel opened up about his daily walk with God on his property. I had pictured my tall, lanky friend in his jeans and boots strolling across acres of land, dodging chickens and plucking carrots. But what he said next caused me to rethink my understanding of how God prepares us for a greater harvest.

"I view the fields through the eyes of harvest," he said. "Is there room for expansion? Can the soil withstand the extra pull on its resources? I must consider these things before I plant any additional seeds. The worst thing I could do is place a seed in soil I have not prepared to receive it. Not only will it cause damage to the soil, but the seed won't produce. So, each day I walk with God, and I ask Him to show me what He sees."

In my love of convenience and ease, I had never had the opportunity to experience cultivation at the level Daniel has experienced. Where I saw soil as something to be brushed off your shoe, he saw it as life and possibility. What was a nuisance to me was a necessity to him. Soil was an incubator in which a seed could thrive. But the soil needs to be ready to ensure the desired outcome—a plentiful harvest. Failure to align the preparation of the soil with the planting of the seed would threaten the harvest.

My failed attempts to follow through on ideas I believed were from God was not a reflection of me being bad soil, but rather unprepared soil. The groundwork had not been laid. I was not adequately prepared to receive the seed. You may not be a homesteader, but perhaps like me, you have attempted to plant a garden or flower bed. Maybe you've grown a few herbs on your windowsill. One of the first things you do is decide what harvest you desire. If you want tomatoes, you must use the correct seeds and choose soil that will yield big, juicy red tomatoes. If you want daffodils, you need daffodil bulbs. You begin with the harvest in mind. You can't control the size of the harvest because it will vary depending on various factors.

Likewise, you can't control the size of the harvest from the seeds God plants either. Yet the condition of the soil remains one of the key factors to a fruitful harvest. God is patient in His preparation of the soil of our lives. He tends to our character, faulty belief systems, unconfessed sin, and deep-rooted iniquity. When we are seeking Him,

He pulls up by the roots anything that would hinder a bigger harvest. And once a field is adequately prepared, He pushes the seed deep into the soil, shines His light on it, and waters it with the rain of His power. When the time is right, the ground shoots forth the blooms of the long-awaited harvest.

The seasons of our lives can be like fields where God cultivates us. He illuminates what is happening within our hearts and shows us more about Himself. These are times of relationship-building that lead us to deeper levels of intimacy. He does not ask us to do more or become more. Rather, the request is for us to become aware of what is being cultivated.

As I've walked with people through their preparation time, I have noticed a recurring set of circumstances that precede planting and harvest. I call these "preparation points" in the journey fields of anointing. We will discuss them more fully in the next chapter. They are areas of becoming that reveal the greater work God is doing in you through your external circumstances.

> Belonging in God's goodness isn't just about feeling His presence in moments of joy. You belong there always. In times of pain and uncertainty, know that His goodness remains constant.

These fields help you identify how you fit in God's redemptive plan. They propel you into belonging. You belong in the goodness of God. You pass through the journey fields of anointing as you wait for God to plant and grow the seeds in you. In these fields, every bloom is a symbol of His love. Every breeze whispers His grace. In the laughter of loved ones and the turning of the seasons, from the monumental to the mundane, you encounter Him and you realize you were made to dwell in His goodness. Belonging in God's goodness isn't just about feeling His presence in moments of joy. You belong there always. In times of pain and uncertainty, know that His goodness remains constant.

Seeing the goodness of God requires recognizing His handiwork. When you train your eyes to see, you'll discover His goodness woven into the fabric of your everyday life. In your busyness, look beyond the surface and see His goodness hovering around you. His provision meeting you in times of need. His grace enveloping you in times of weakness. Allow His goodness to anchor your soul in His unchanging character. Declare His goodness in the face of adversity, standing firm on the assurance that He is with you, guiding you, and loving you through every storm. These fields invite you to receive the unlimited good available to you.

Belonging in God's Goodness

Psalm 23:6 — "Surely your goodness and love will follow me all the days of my life, and I will dwell in the house of the LORD forever."

Practical application — Trust in God's goodness. Remind yourself daily that His goodness is ever-present, regardless of circumstances. Find your place of belonging in the assurance of God's unfailing

goodness toward you. Let this truth embolden you. Live with confident contentment.

Psalm 100:5 — "For the LORD is good and his love endures forever;
his faithfulness continues through all generations."

Practical application — Your family also belongs in the goodness of
God. Share stories of God's goodness with your children and relatives.
Take every opportunity to share your God story. Reflect on specific
instances where you've experienced His goodness, love, and faithfulness. Thank Him for extending His goodness through all generations
of your bloodline.

James 1:17 — "Every good and perfect gift is from above, coming
down from the Father of the heavenly lights, who does not change like
shifting shadows."

Practical application — Develop a habit of seeing the goodness of
God around you. Consider keeping a journal to record the good gifts
you receive from God each day. Draw near to Him. Turn to the truth
of His Word. Behold Him. Open your eyes to His wonders. Immerse
yourself in His presence. Experience the fullness He offers, and
remember you belong in the goodness of God, now and forevermore.

Daily Unveiling

1. What is being cultivated during the current season
   of your life?

2. When you look at your life as a field, what is the harvest you anticipate?

3. Goodness is a constant companion in your life. Pray this simple gratitude prayer: "God, thank You for Your goodness."

Chapter 17

UNEARTHED POTENTIAL

I used to hear church people declare that someone was anointed after that person sang a beautiful solo or finished preaching a rousing sermon. Naturally, I associated the anointing with personal talent or a form of showmanship one can learn. I now believe anointing has nothing to do with one's talent or ability to perform. It is not the training of a skill but the yielding of a field. Now when I reference the anointing in someone's life, I'm not praising their talent but acknowledging their willingness to allow the influence of the Holy Spirit to be expressed through their abilities. Their life has become permeable to the power of God in such a way that it is affecting all who experience it with the same power that raised Jesus from the dead.

In the same way that anointing oil was used throughout the Bible marking things as set apart or holy, an anointed life is made distinct by the power and authority of God's work within us.

As a carrier of the Holy Spirit, you house His sanctifying influence even during pressure-filled seasons. It is in the pressing that you release an expression of heaven on the earth. One of the definitions I love comes from Smith's Bible Dictionary, which says anointing "expresses the sanctifying influences of the Holy Spirit upon Christians who are priests and kings unto God."[1] In 2 Corinthians 1:21–22, we learn that when we receive salvation, we are immediately indwelt by the Holy Spirit and joined to Christ, the Anointed One.

When I talk about "fields of anointing," I'm not speaking of fields of olive trees where the fruit will one day be pressed to make oil. In these anointing fields I'm talking about, you get pressed. I realize that probably doesn't sound like fun (and I can confirm it is not), but it produces a harvest of great value.

There are four anointing fields: suffering, surrendering, stretching, and soaring. Each field has pressure, produces fruit, and has a purpose. Do not think of these fields as sequential ladder rungs where you climb from suffering up to soaring. You could find yourself lingering in a field for a prolonged period, and then, in the blink of an eye, find yourself in any other field. Life is unpredictable and constantly changing. In one day, suffering can be met by a miracle, leaving you soaring on the wind of answered prayer. The stretching field can ask more of you than you are willing to give, so you find yourself in the field of surrendering first. These aren't destinations to strive to achieve. They are experiences embedded in the process of becoming more aware of how God is moving in and through you.

As you look at each field of anointing, think about which of these fields you are in now. You may find yourself in more than one of them at once. Where is the sanctifying influence of the Holy Spirit showing up in your life? How have you been divinely equipped to show Jesus to the world? In which fields do you find it easier to work with God? In which fields do you tend to work against Him? What judgments about yourself and about God have you attached to each field?

The harvest produced in each field is worth the preparation and the pressing. We need more of the Holy Spirit in every area of our lives. Learning how to navigate the pressure with God is the most direct route to producing the desired fruit and releasing the anointing in our lives. In doing so, we move past our natural limitations and can see the unearthed potential available to us within each of these fields.

Fields of Anointing
The Field of Suffering

No one enjoys this field. It's a barren place void of the color, mirth, and vitality we long to enjoy. Pain is near, often along with its companions: anxiety, sorrow, and illness. Growing in this field requires perseverance. Romans 5:3–5 puts it this way: "Not only so, but we also glory in our sufferings, because we know that suffering produces perseverance; perseverance, character; and character, hope. And hope does not put us to shame, because God's love has been poured out into our hearts through the Holy Spirit, who has been given to us."

If you allow the seed of God's Word to grow in the field of suffering, it will produce the fruit of hope. Not a flimsy hope that becomes shredded at the first hint of stormy weather, but a stronghold of hope. A level of hope that is not easily swayed by external circumstances. We hear a lot of talk about breaking free from negative strongholds, but hope is a beneficial stronghold to which you want to cling.

Zechariah 9:12 declares, "Return to your stronghold, O prisoners of hope; today I declare that I will restore to you double" (ESV). Sometimes the thing you lost is doubled, and other times your strength to persevere is doubled. But there is always a harvest from this field.

The Field of Surrendering

This next field is for those who struggle with patience. If you frequently find yourself trapped on the interstate behind a car in the far-left lane going exactly the speed limit, or if you tend to always choose the slowest line at the grocery store, I may be talking to you. I spent years in this field. Patience does not come naturally to me. I'm a doer and doers don't do patience. Point me in the direction of the action, please.

I relate to the stories in the Bible about those who got tired of waiting on God and took matters into their own hands, such as the parable of the prodigal son who demanded his inheritance early rather than waiting for it to be passed down to him. Consider Abraham and Sarah deciding they didn't need God to help them have a baby. Why wait for Sarah's womb to open when there was a servant woman who could bear Abraham a child right now? The result of their impatience is still evident in the unrest and warring happening between the offspring of their two heirs.

> Surrendering to God's timing is not punishment—it's positioning. Surrender produces within you the power to possess the promise God's way.

And what about when Saul, tired of waiting on Samuel to come fulfill his priestly duty, performed the sacrificial offering himself? This directly contradicted God's specific guidelines. In fact, after learning of Saul's actions, Samuel lamented, "You have not kept the command the LORD your God gave you; if you had, he would have established your kingdom over Israel for all time" (1 Sam. 13:13). Through his impatience, Saul tragically misses out on lifelong generational blessings.

Surrendering to God's timing is not punishment—it's positioning. Surrendering produces within you the power to possess the promise God's way. We may be able to produce a variation of the promise through our own power, but it will not carry the power of God. It will be a smaller, diminished version of what is possible. Listen to the encouragement found in Psalm 37:7–9: "Be still before the LORD and wait patiently for him; do not fret when people succeed in their ways, when they carry out their wicked schemes. Refrain from anger and turn from wrath; do not fret—it leads only to evil. For those who are evil will be destroyed, but those who hope in the LORD will inherit the land."

I don't want a counterfeit version of the promise. I would rather wait for God's appointed time for the promise to be fulfilled. I would rather surrender quick gratification for lasting satisfaction. Habakkuk 2:3 puts it this way: "For the vision is yet for the appointed [future] time it hurries toward the goal [of fulfillment]; it will not fail. Even though it delays, wait [patiently] for it, because it will certainly come; it will not delay" (AMP). This field can seem like one long postponement, but the fruit produced will be rightly established and will remain.

The Field of Stretching

This field is for those who wrestle with unbelief. It requires us to confront our stand on what is possible. The field of stretching leads us into places of greater capacity in our faith. God has no limit to His capacity. Limits lie in our unbelief. In the field of stretching, our unbelief is expanded into new heights of trust. This field allows us to push through doubt and allow God to supersede our logic and move in supernatural ways. Picture drawing a circle on a piece of paper. Imagine that inside the circle exist your rational thoughts on how something can be accomplished. Outside the circle exists all the ways God could accomplish it. No matter how big you draw the circle, there will always be space around it. The larger the space outside of your circle of reasoning, the more open you are to what is possible with God!

Consider the different moments in Scripture where people experienced stretching. Moses brought the Israelites out of Egypt to a sea too great for them to swim across. God asked Moses to stretch out his staff to the Red Sea. The situation looked impossible, but stretching out his arm was an act of faith that God could work a miracle outside of Moses's circle of understanding. In the New Testament, we observe Jesus asking people with leprosy to stretch out their hands, turning their inward faith and outward obedience into possibility. The woman with an issue of blood said to herself, "Let me stretch out and touch the hem of His garment." The stretching preceded the possibility of her healing. Her capacity for faith is what Jesus declared healed her. It wasn't simply the act of stretching but the woman's inner confidence in the Savior. Stretching allows you to acknowledge the vast possibility of what God can do.

You may not have a sea to cross or leprosy you need healed. Today, your stretching may look different. When your bank account is running low, and you feel prompted to tithe, it's a stretch. When you feel led to start a business or ministry and you're afraid of what people will say, it's a stretch. When your spouse of forty years dies, and your whole world was built around that person, it's a stretch. Whether in your career, ministry, family, health, or relationships, you will feel stretched many times throughout your life. When you feel this pull, respond like the woman who touched the hem of Jesus' robe. Stretch out your hand in faith and access the possibilities of what God can do in your situation.

Miracles don't happen without stretching. If you've found yourself saying, "God, I don't know how You're going to do it," you are in the field of stretching. Remember the words of Mark 10:27: "Jesus looked at them and said, 'With man this is impossible, but not with God; all things are possible with God.'" Wonders and miracles arise from the field of stretching as we reach out to a God who can do anything.

The Field of Soaring

This field can be a challenging one for those of us who fight against God's call to rest. Soaring is a form of flight that some large birds use to travel great distances without exerting a lot of energy. Through soaring, some can travel for days barely flapping their wings. They gain altitude and travel using the air currents in the atmosphere. They are moved by the wind. When we are in the field of soaring, we are moved along by the wind of God's Spirit.

Ruach is the Hebrew word for breath, wind, or spirit. In Genesis, it is used to describe the Spirit of God. The word denotes more of a life-sustaining essence than a physical force. Unlike a beachside breeze that causes your hair to fly in every direction at once, this type of wind is a lifting wind that produces strength. Isaiah 40:31 says, "But those who hope in the LORD will renew their strength. They will soar on wings like eagles; they will run and not grow weary, they will walk and not be faint." "Mount up" means to ascend, to climb, or to go higher. In the waiting, in the pausing, in the resting, you ascend on Holy Spirit power.

Just as an eagle can soar for miles using a small amount energy, there will be times when you can accomplish way more than humanly possible through God's power. People will ask you questions like, "How do you do it all? What's the secret?" And the only truthful answer you can give is, "I don't know." In your field of soaring, many may marvel at your fruitfulness and strength. As you rest on the wind of the Spirit, it gives you sustainable power to go farther and longer without having to flap around expending as much energy. This doesn't mean you are sitting around doing nothing. Soaring requires focus and active participation with the Spirit of God.

Some of the fields of anointing are interconnected. When birds soar, their wings must be fully extended. This is a picture of both stretching and soaring. Suffering can lead us into surrendering. And surrendering gives us the ability to stretch our faith and move into a place of greater trust in Him. You can move around these fields in any sequence. Notice that each field has pressures and challenges. Pressure is a normal part of a fallen world. Jesus told us in John 16:33, "In the world you will have tribulation" (ESV). Tribulation is derived from the Latin *tribulare*, which means "press" or "oppress." Jesus didn't say you *may* have tribulation; He said you *will* have it. Pressure is a part of the process. It is guaranteed. When we accept the role of pressure in God's good work in our lives, we can stop fighting it and learn to let the anointing flow. Even in times of immense pressure, we can be empowered by the Holy Spirit. Pressure exists both in success and failure; you will feel pressed by both. Hold to the knowledge that each field produces a harvest. You are coming out more equipped, more prepared, and more like Jesus.

Whether suffering, surrendering, stretching, or soaring, thank God for the field of preparation in which you find yourself. You may not be in a season you would choose, but anointing comes with a promise: fruit. The world is full of people needing to be fully known. Once you have spent time in these fields, it's time to take that anointing out into the world.

When Jesus was on the earth, He traveled through towns and villages preaching the gospel and healing people of sickness and disease. Matthew 9:36–38 describes Jesus' response:

> When he saw the crowds, he had compassion on them, because they were harassed and helpless, like sheep without a shepherd. Then he said to his disciples, "The harvest is plentiful but the workers are few. Ask the Lord of the harvest, therefore, to send out workers into his harvest field."

When you have traveled through the fields of suffering, surrendering, stretching, and soaring, you will more freely express the Holy

Spirit's influence and be able to point others to a life-giving relationship with Christ.

Belonging in God's Faithfulness

1 Corinthians 1:9 — "God is faithful, who has called you into fellowship with his Son, Jesus Christ our Lord."

Practical application — God has promised to never leave nor forsake you. Cultivate a daily practice of meditation on His persistent faithfulness. Seek intimacy with God knowing He is faithful to draw near to those who seek Him. Find strength in His constant presence.

Hebrews 10:23 — "Let us hold unswervingly to the hope we profess, for he who promised is faithful."

Practical application — Your hope belongs in an unwavering, promise-keeping God. Confidently hold onto His Word regardless of trials that arise. Remind yourself of God's faithfulness by memorizing Scriptures that carry promises that apply to your circumstances.

Psalm 89:8 — "Who is like you, LORD God Almighty? You, LORD, are mighty, and your faithfulness surrounds you."

Practical application — Find belonging in the greatness of God's faithfulness, knowing it encamps around Him. Every aspect of His being testifies to His awesomeness. He has no rival. Walk boldly into today, recognizing there is no one like your God.

Daily Unveiling

1. Which of the four fields—suffering, surrendering, stretching, or soaring—do you find yourself in today?

2. How are your beliefs about life's challenges and pressures changing?

3. Pressure is part of God's process of sanctification. Pray this simple prayer: "God, release the expression of the Holy Spirit within me."

Chapter 18

UNASHAMED EXPOSURE

Every day holds opportunities to encounter the sacred. On one random day at the hospital, the opportunity came in the form of chestnut brown eyes. In an instant, an ordinary workday transformed into something holy. I stepped into a sacred space where the broken lay themselves down to become a living sacrifice. A space where they stand naked and unashamed, exposed and fully known.

That morning I had rushed with a medical team to the ambulance bay as the high-pitched squeal of sirens drew near. The doors of the ambulance burst open, and a woman lay motionless on the gurney, unaware of the cacophony of activity whirling around her.

"She's not breathing," came the brief assessment from the emergency medical service leader.

The team jumped into action, checking her vital signs, rolling the gurney into a triage room, and preparing her for intubation. They did what they were trained to do with one goal—to support life and bring it back to this woman. Each of us blocked out distractions, focusing on our patient. It's no wonder I didn't see him—the woman's husband. I'm sure he was there the whole time … watching, praying, hoping.

Nobody knew how long the woman had been down. Her husband had found her lying on the bathroom floor after returning from the park with their son. He and his son had spent the morning enjoying slides and swings, not knowing life was about to take them on an unwanted detour.

"Time of death, 2:58 p.m."

The words came thirty minutes after the ambulance arrived. We stepped back from the woman's lifeless body. I removed my gloves. My emotions remained suspended in time, captivated by the intricate dance of life and death and by the finality of it all. In one unforeseen moment, an artery blocked, and that was it. It didn't matter that she was in her mid-thirties. It didn't matter that she had no previous health issues. Today was her day to transition from this life to the next.

Suddenly, I noticed her husband standing in the far corner of the room. The flurry of activity had concealed his presence. But now, in the stillness, he approached her bedside. He reached out to touch her and stopped short, covering his face with his hands, and sinking to the floor. Staff members tried to comfort him, but you can't console the inconsolable. Kind words wouldn't bring her back. He cried out in anguish, vocalizing his pain for us all. The beeping ceased as a nurse turned off the monitor. The only sound left in the room was one of heartbreak.

That's when I saw him, a boy no more than five years old with beautiful chestnut brown eyes. He had been in the family room with a nurse, rushing in at the sound of his father's wailing. His flip-flopped feet slapped against the hospital floor as he sprinted toward the door. I jumped in his path just in time. There was no way I was going to let him see his lifeless mother on that table barely dressed with tubes down her throat. There was no way I was going to have this image impressed in his mind. We couldn't save her, but we could shield him from the horror of this scene. He had every right to see his mother and say his goodbyes, but not like this.

"I want my mama!" he demanded, his small fist at his side, tears streaming down his face.

I'm not sure exactly what it looks like to daily take up your cross, but I suddenly felt that this was a cross I was meant to bear. Who best to show comfort to the motherless than someone who had experienced it? Who best to shield the heart of a hurting child than someone who has been hurt? Who best to point to the light in the darkness than someone who has walked through that same darkness? I knew his pain well because I had lived it. It was as if God had given me a chance to do for him what I wished someone had done for me.

I stood firm, willing to withstand his anger and ready to intercept his pain. But I wasn't prepared for what came next. The little boy plowed into my legs with an intensity that made me stumble backwards. He wrapped his arms around both my calves, squeezing with all his might and letting out a mournful cry that unraveled any thread of composure left in the room. The sound tore through me. It pulled the rip cord of my checked emotions. It uprooted everything I believed about the work I do. I had always viewed the practice of medicine as beginning and ending with the patient. On this day, I realized the higher work in this situation was not trying to revive a body that had been dead for hours before arriving to the ER but to revive two souls that had to keep living.

Sacred Spaces

Medical school doesn't train you for these things; nothing does. We don't take classes on how to love people well or study lessons on compassion. We acquire this knowledge in the day-to-day of living in a broken world. Through life, we learn to protect our hearts. We want to shield them from being hurt and guard them against future pain. But ... there are times when your need to protect your heart is superseded by an unexplainable, divine pull. In these moments, your past hurts, pain, and current struggles open you up like a blooming flower. One at a time, the petals of your heart are pulled back by the Master to release the fragrance of fully giving yourself.

When that little boy grabbed my legs, I truly began to understand there is a difference between the work we do because we are trained to do it and the sacred spaces we have the opportunities to work in with God. The two may converge, but in understanding our sacred calling, we break free into the wide open space of living fully and loving boldly.

Most of our waking hours are spent doing work of some kind. Much of it may seem mundane, ordinary, and uninspired. This leads us to devalue the work and, ultimately, ourselves. We begin to feel like interchangeable parts, becoming overly preoccupied by what we do and losing focus on why we do it. We fail to recognize the sacred spaces where we can do our most important work—work that God has prepared for us to do. Everyone has sacred work assigned to them.

Sacred spaces are the moments that invite you to do the God-ordained work only you can do. I was keenly aware that as a person who had lost my mother, I was the right person to comfort that young boy. God had placed me in that room for that very moment. Sacred spaces often present themselves as eerily coincidental circumstances. Moments when you happen to be in the right place at the right time or meet the right person. Times when your abilities and experience position you for an opportunity you could not have orchestrated on your own.

Instead of dipping our toes into these sacred spaces, if we plunge into the deep end and allow them to cover us, we will become dissatisfied living in the shallows. Sacred spaces disrupt our ability to stay ankle-deep when there is a deeply gratifying life waiting to wash over us.

I have always viewed the job I do to earn a living as my secular work. My job was the labor I did to have some type of enjoyable existence when the work was done. As a medical professional, it was easy to see the value in helping people get healthier, but I viewed it as transactional, not transformational. Doctoring was temporal work with no significant effect on the eternal and no connection to the spiritual. I approached it as a career and not a calling. That mindset kept me locked in discontentment for so long, I stopped looking for a way to escape. I settled into the belief that I was not one of the chosen few called to do sacred work. I mistakenly believed that I had to choose between the sacred and the secular. Ministry or medicine? I could do one or the other, but not both.

The belief that only ministers and missionaries are called to do spiritual work has left a vacancy of Spirit-led laborers in many fields that need their presence, their influence, and their gifts.

This seeming division caused a tug-of-war in my heart. A fierce battle between a cultural paradigm and a simple spiritual principle that tells me whatever work I do should be done as if I were working for the Lord (Col. 3:23–24). The division I had created in my mind was not from the Lord. Sacred work is not reserved for those in vocational ministry such as pastors and missionaries. The work they do is sacred, but full-time ministry is only one type of sacred work. The belief that only ministers and missionaries are called to do spiritual work has left a vacancy of Spirit-led laborers in many fields that need their presence, their influence, and their gifts.

What would happen if you integrated your faith into every sphere of your life—relationships, job, hobbies, finances, health? What would happen if God was able to move freely in the different fields where you have influence—in business, government, education, entertainment, health care, churches, and in your home? The Lord invites you to tear down the walls between the sacred and secular. Welcome Him into it all. Remove the boundaries you've created in your mind regarding what qualifies as "spiritual work" and consider that it is *all* spiritual work. Resist the temptation to predetermine where God will move next.

Sacred Work

I am not a fan of the term "work-life balance." We act as if life and work are two antagonistic forces. One pulling us up and the other pulling us down. In our attempt to not be pulled in two, we have tried to balance these forces, a task that is futile because they were never meant to exist in balance. I have discovered that you cannot place your life on one side of the scales and your work on the other and expect to experience any level of satisfaction. Work and life cannot be balanced, but they can function in harmony. Through integration of the two, you can experience greater freedom, peace, and satisfaction. They can coexist without the tension of one being more worthy or important than the other. They can reside in a place of quiet confidence, trust, and rest.

For the past two years, I have shared with thousands of people through my book *Sacred Rest* about how they can get the rest they need. I would be remiss if I do not also share the reason why rest is not just for your personal benefit. It is part of the preparation for you to do the deeper work of serving God and others well. Rest is how God sensitizes us to the sacred offering within our work.

During the writing of *Sacred Rest*, I spent an entire year studying Genesis. This is where God first introduced the concept of rest. But He also revealed the relationship between rest and work. I'm sure you've heard the creation story many times, but familiarity with a section of Scripture can anesthetize your sensitivity to its life-changing power. I didn't spend a year studying Genesis because I couldn't get enough of it. No, I diligently studied this one book because I sensed I was missing something. When the light bulb eventually came on, it changed my perception of work and rest.

In the creation account, we learn that on the sixth day God created all the creatures on the earth and then created mankind in His own image. "God blessed them and said to them, 'Be fruitful and increase in number; fill the earth and subdue it. Rule over the fish in the sea and the birds in the sky and over every living creature that moves on the ground" (Gen. 1:28). The following day, God rested. Have you ever thought about what Adam and Eve were doing while God was resting? We can only assume they were resting too.

Humankind's first full day on the earth was a day of rest. There is no mention of work until after the day of rest (Gen. 2:15). God created mankind, informed them of the work to be done, and then gifted them a time of rest before sending them out to do the work. For years I thought I had to work to earn rest. That's not true. God's pattern is for me to do my work from a place of rest.

This was a life-altering realization. It was the permission I had been seeking and the license I needed to rest well. It was an invitation to live with nothing to prove and everything to give. I recognized in this truth an opportunity to work not only from my places of greatest strength but also from my places of greatest weakness. I felt the Lord inviting me to willingly bring everything I am and everything I am not and lay them both before Him as a sacrifice to be poured out. I sensed a holy call to do sacred work.

As we have previously discussed, sacred work consists of Spirit-inspired activities that impact those around you in meaningful ways. This work is not validated by the number of letters in front of or behind your name. Nor is it dependent on the number of people affected. It is not limited by your education or your financial situation. Sacred work stands available to all who want to cooperate with the Holy Spirit to leave the places they inhabit better than they found them. It's available to everyone who desires to use their gifts, skills, and talents to their full potential in every area of life.

Sacred work exposes you to the pain of the world, and in the process, you become more like Jesus. You weep for what moves His heart;

you bend toward the broken as a vessel of His compassion. You care for the hurting. His Spirit empowers you to step into their pain unafraid and unashamed. He uses you to be peace in another's storm. Through sacred work, you discover where you fit in God's plan to bring healing and wholeness to the world.

Belonging in God's Peace

Philippians 4:6–7 — "Do not be anxious about anything, but in every situation, by prayer and petition, with thanksgiving, present your requests to God. And the peace of God, which transcends all understanding, will guard your hearts and your minds in Christ Jesus."

Practical application — Cultivate a habit of prayerful intercession for others, bringing their worries and concerns to God. Peace is a place where everyone belongs. Practice solitude and quiet waiting as you calm your mind and heart before God. Shift your perspective to His presence and open your heart to receive His peace.

John 14:27 — "Peace I leave with you; my peace I give you. I do not give to you as the world gives. Do not let your hearts be troubled and do not be afraid."

Practical application — Meditate on Jesus' promise of peace and allow His words to dwell richly in your heart. When faced with fear or anxiety, intentionally choose to trust in His peace, which surpasses worldly understanding and provides comfort and assurance. Plunge into peace as one would dive into the deep end of a pool. Let it overtake you.

Colossians 3:15 — "Let the peace of Christ rule in your hearts, since as members of one body you were called to peace. And be thankful."

Practical application — Invite the peace of Christ to rule and reign in your heart. Surrender control and allow His peace to guide your thoughts, decisions, and interactions with others. Strive to have a humble spirit, recognizing God in you is the hope of glory.

Daily Unveiling

1. How do you experience sacred rest—exploring the outdoors, having a time of reflection, journaling, taking a nap?
2. When have you felt like you were doing sacred work?
3. Every day is an opportunity to experience the sacred. Pray this simple prayer: "God, invite me into a sacred space today."

Chapter 19

UNFINISHED BUSINESS

You can be busy at work without your work being beneficial to you or others. There are days when I'm working intently on a task or striving to complete a project without paying attention to the greater purpose of the assignment. I can spend time in meetings where I am physically present and accounted for without being accountable to those in the room by being attentive and engaging with the conversation. Hours occupied clearing my inbox or replying to messages without any depth of thought or feeling are allocated just for the sake of checking off another box on my to-do list.

The key to a healthy relationship with work lies in recognizing when you have defaulted to busy work. We do these ritualistic activities because they must be done, and sometimes we do them without allowing our head and heart to engage with what our hands are doing. We are in action without being motivated to act. Yet, it is in these moments that sacred work often presents itself.

Perhaps you've had an experience where you were liberated from the habitual and were able to see the spiritual and eternal potential of the moment. When this happens, our hearts recognize the need for a change and redirect our hands to release the familiar and reach for the unknown. A routine meeting can turn into a ministry opportunity. Replying to a message can become a chance to authentically show up and shift the course of someone's day.

Sacred work occurs in the present because this is where the Holy Spirit dwells. It is doing the inspired assignment that is before you. That assignment is very personal to each of us. Our inspirations arise from our past experiences, joys, hurts, loves, losses, and successes. You are the only one who can do the sacred work you are called to do.

Sacred work does not seek attention, promotion, or recognition. It flows from the heart of God. It is intentionally helpful, radically loving, and openly uplifting. At times it sits quietly, awaiting the right moment to interject peace, hope, and healing. At other times it storms the gates, roaring with power, conviction, and authority.

This work is not taught in classrooms or textbooks. Sacred work is pushed out through the pain of walking through the darkness and birthed out of an intimate relationship with a Holy God. It arises in the beholding, becoming, and belonging. From this labor, you emerge exposed and vulnerable. Your mind surrenders its questions, your heart opens wide, and your hands reach out. Sacred work deposits you in a new place of understanding of who God is and the greatness of His power at work in and through you.

Your busy work may define what you do on the outside, but sacred work reveals who you are on the inside. You could be in your office working when a colleague walks in to discuss a problem she's having on a project. Her demeanor and words suggest she does not feel capable of accomplishing the task. In that moment you have a choice. You can focus on the busy work to ensure the task is accomplished. Or you can redirect to the sacred work of building her confidence. Or you could be cooking dinner for the family when your son comes in and sits at the counter to do homework. His furrowed brow and clenched jaw convey he is struggling with the assignment. You have a choice. You can continue the busy work of prepping the meal or redirect to accomplish the sacred work of being emotionally available to your teen.

The busy work will not go away, but it does not have to stop you from engaging in the sacred work God has called you to. Both kinds of work can operate in tandem to accomplish a more significant outcome. Busy work is planned, ritualistic, and familiar. Busy work is the set of tasks you've been trained to do and are expected of you. When done exclusively, busy work can leave you feeling drained and depleted. Sacred work is spontaneous, creative, and unfamiliar. It can be uncomfortable because it demands that you draw from the resources you have gathered on your journey. It also requires vulnerability and transparency. Sacred work inserts you into a moment where you have what someone else needs because you have a deep personal understanding.

Busy work produces an external result. Sacred work initiates an internal change. The conscious mind is an amazing thing. Once you understand this principle of deeper work, your mind will attempt to help you seek it out. Suddenly, it may seem like every part of your day becomes a potential occasion for sacred work. Remember that sacred work is God-directed and Spirit-led. Your role is not to create moments, but to be willing and available when they present themselves.

I spent most of my career seeing these moments as interruptions that kept me from getting my "real" work done. My work defined me, and I didn't like who it declared me to be. It showed me to be a person more concerned with action than with people, more focused on outcomes than opportunities, more motivated by getting things accomplished for God than getting to know God's heart. In the process, I found myself spending over forty hours each week doing work that drained the life out of me when all along I had the power to recover my life. I had the power to choose to accept the sacred work before me and trust that the busy work would get done. In my acceptance, I commenced on an exciting, humbling, joyful journey to be fully known and become the person I truly am.

Finding Your Sacred Work

Sacred work cannot be replicated by the people around you. No one can do your work with the same level of offering that you can give because no one has walked your personal journey with God. That unexplainable "something" that flows from your natural identity and relationship with God makes you the right person in that moment to do a particular work. It is an extra something that is not taught but cultivated from the inside.

Doing sacred work requires you to go deep into your "why"—your motivation for living the way you do. Perhaps you have a heart for justice for the downtrodden. Maybe you care deeply about passing on faith to the next generation. Or you may have a passion for nutrition and physical fitness as tools to steward the body God has given you. Every person's why will be different.

It also requires you to go deep into your "why not" because you must define what you view as sacred or most important. What values, qualities, principles, and truths echo who God is in your life? Are they worth protecting? Do they inspire awe inside of you? Are you willing to offer your head, heart, and hands to share them?

Once you identify your unwavering beliefs and values, you identify the key to enjoying work you are uniquely gifted to do with a level of excellence that goes beyond your level of training. Sacred work demands your gifts and talents come forth in a way that brings value to the world around you. It also unlocks areas of satisfaction you have yet to enjoy.

When asked about what motivates her work with young women, my friend Gail replied, "Love is my 'why.' I've spent much of my life longing for it. I've sought it out with people who confused it with lust. I've resisted it from people with good intentions. Finding true love has been my lifelong quest because part of me has always wondered if I am unlovable.

"Now I think, 'Why not me with a loving husband?'" she continued. "'Why not me as God's beloved?' Not only am I lovable but I can be a conduit of His love to others everywhere I go. From my conversations with friends to the projects I complete at work, it's all done from a place of love."

At this time in history, when sacred work is needed more than ever, fewer people are pursuing it. It's easier to show up for the daily grind, put in the hours, and collect a check. It's easier but it does not make life easy. Busy work is a sure path to a slow death to the gifts, talents, and calling placed within you. Busyness keeps you spiritually disconnected from the work of your hands and the abundant life God desires for you to live. As you make room for sacred work, don't be surprised when dormant gifts spring to life.

If you have spent years on the job in a secular environment where you have not integrated your faith, incorporating the sacred can feel threatening. Sometimes a secular job with all its titles and trimmings can become attached to your identity. You suppress expression of your natural identity beyond what is needed for the job. You bypass the joyful satisfaction you could experience because you limit who you are becoming and deny yourself access to places where you belong.

The journey of stepping into the fullness of your identity is rarely a linear one. It involves a process of letting go of old identities and embracing new ones. It took me three years of wrestling with God before I finally surrendered to His process of beholding, becoming, and belonging. There was unfinished business God had for me, and I am thankful for His faithfulness to remain in the process with me. I had to be still long enough to behold Him beholding me. The revelation of the unfinished business God had for me began with four words: "This season is over."

God has never spoken audibly to me. The scientific part of my brain would probably spontaneously combust if that happened, but I often hear the still, small voice of His Spirit. One day while at my medical practice, I heard the words: "This season is over." Instinctively, I knew the season in question was practicing clinical medicine. I thought to myself, *This must be the enemy messing with me because there is no way God would be asking me to walk away from the only career I know—the work I am trained to do.* I pushed the message as far down in my conscious mind as possible and continued to work the job I'd spent seven years training to do.

Once God speaks, change will occur. For twenty years I worked in clinical medicine and loved every minute of it. The high adrenaline days after the Southeastern Conference football games when swarms of people would come in with chest pain. The slow lull of the holiday season when even the sickest patients would sign out against medical advice to be home with their families for Christmas. Busy or slow, being a doctor was my life and it brought me joy. After I heard—and ignored—the words, "This season is over," joy seemed to vanish. And people noticed.

Nurses asked if I was okay when they noticed the absence of my usual sunny disposition. I snapped at people unnecessarily and had no patience for errors. Neither I nor the work was the same. As God was gently prodding me toward what was next, it seemed as if His favor at my current job had lifted. Maybe I was a bit like Jonah when he ran away to Tarshish. I didn't feel like I was walking in disobedience; I thought I was being reasonable. Surely, I had heard wrong.

Something I learned from that season is that when the cloud of God's glory moves, move with it. Being in unfamiliar territory with God's grace is much better than being in the familiar without it. I had not yet taken hold of the power of Psalm 46:10. I did not know how to be still, and I had so much to learn about knowing God in His fullness.

The only thing I knew to do was seek Him in prayer for further instructions. "I hear You, God," I prayed, "but I don't know how that's going to work. I've spent literally my entire life working toward this one thing. This white coat is my identity!" As soon as I prayed those words, the Holy Spirit spoke to my heart: "And that's the reason you need to take it off. It was never meant to be your identity."

When the cloud of God's glory moves,
move with it. Being in unfamiliar territory
with God's grace is much better than
being in the familiar without it.

I now realize my white coat was only supposed to be part of my armor for a season. It was the armor for one of the arenas in which God placed me—*for a season*. Now my armor looks different. So do my arenas. They fit the current season I am in with God. I still carry the wisdom, skill, and talents from seasons past, but He is repurposing them to accomplish His will in and through me. There was unfinished business God had for me to do, and it required me to break past my comfort zone and launch into a new, scary adventure with Him. This is the sacred journey He is inviting you into. Don't stop with the identity you've grown comfortable with. Let God reveal all of who you are as He walks with you into new territory.

Romans tells us the gifts and callings of God are "irrevocable" (Rom. 11:29 ESV). They may remain dormant for a time, but eventually the rain will fall on them and sprouts will appear. They will push their way through doubt. They will shove aside fear. The sprouts will shoot up through the darkness and stretch toward the light of day, reminding you of the untapped potential that remains. Potential that has been reserved for this time, this season, this moment. Now is not the time to avoid the rain by hiding beneath the umbrella of your white coat. Now is the time to stand in the rain. Let it fall on you and saturate the places you've been guarding. Let the rain create new growth as the Lord leads you to the sacred work awaiting you. Let it awaken the gifts within like new blooms opening to the sun.

Belonging in God's Blessing

2 Corinthians 9:8 — "And God is able to bless you abundantly, so that in all things at all times, having all that you need, you will abound in every good work."

Practical application — Behold the promise of God's abundant blessings that overflow in every aspect of your life. Trust that you belong in God's provision and know He can meet all your needs. Live with confidence, knowing God's blessings enable you to make a positive impact in the world around you. Embrace each day with an abounding spirit ready to share God's blessings with others.

Deuteronomy 28:2 — "All these blessings will come on you and accompany you if you obey the LORD your God."

Practical application — Obey God's commands and align your life with His will, knowing His blessings follow those who walk in obedience. Seek to live a life of righteousness and integrity, trusting that God's blessings will accompany you on your journey.

Ephesians 1:3 — "Praise be to the God and Father of our Lord Jesus Christ, who has blessed us in the heavenly realms with every spiritual blessing in Christ."

Practical application — Become aware of the spiritual blessings that are yours in Christ Jesus. Spend time beholding the King of Kings. Praise God for the blessings He has lavished on you including salvation, forgiveness, and the indwelling presence of the Holy Spirit.

Daily Unveiling

1. What activities in your life have become busy work?
2. Is there something God is asking you to let go of to make room for something new?
3. Blessings flow when we are in the right spiritual alignment. Pray this simple prayer: "God, whisper the divine insight I need to know."

Chapter 20

FULLY KNOWN

The book of Esther in the Old Testament is the story of one woman's journey to being fully known. Esther was a young Jewish orphan being cared for by her cousin Mordecai in Persia following the exile. The Bible does not give any details about her parents' deaths. Nor do we know how she came to live with her cousin. The big shift in her story occurs when King Xerxes decides he is ready for a new wife. He sends his officials throughout the land to gather the most beautiful women and bring them to the palace.

That is how Esther became a candidate to be the new queen. Before the women were presented to the king, they had to undergo a time of intense preparation. Only after this process would they be given their opportunity to impress the king. Esther's one night turned into a lifetime when King Xerxes selected her as his queen. And in that role, Esther found her greater life purpose. She had been divinely positioned to save not only her cousin but also her people, the Jews.

As far as we can determine, Esther's childhood was marked by pain—as an orphan, she may have experienced the pain of loss and abandonment. I imagine her as content living with Mordecai, not looking for a God-sized adventure. In fact, God's name is never mentioned in the book of Esther. We aren't told that this young Jewish woman had any big dreams or aspirations.

Without warning, Esther was forced to leave the familiar place she had known her whole life. The identity she had known being raised by Mordecai was erased, a page was turned, and a new story began to be written. She was recognized as someone who had the potential to be a queen. God saw an aptitude for increased capacity. He saw the beauty despite the scars. He saw a fertile field where He could cultivate a new and extraordinary identity. He saw a future queen who would be willing to sacrifice her life for her people. He saw something in Esther that required unveiling.

There is purpose in the unveiling: the pulling back of everything that conceals the fullness of your identity. It can be an event or a process—however God chooses to orchestrate your being fully known journey. It is a time of beholding, becoming, and belonging. In the story of Esther, we watch an unveiling of the young woman's identity. From the moment she arrived at the palace, Esther experienced favor and was positioned in the "best place in the harem" (Est. 2:9). Esther's unveiling occurred over a period of years that began with a twelve-month beautification process.

The Hebrew noun used to describe Esther's treatments is derived from a verb that means "to polish, scrape, or rub," implying an exfoliation treatment.[1] This aligns with the concept of purification. This was a time of sloughing off the old so new healthy cells could surface. As you go through an unveiling process, parts of your identity must be scraped away to allow for regeneration. Old beliefs must be rubbed out so your mind can be renewed. Wounds and scars must be polished with healing oils.

Olive oil and myrrh were the oils used during the first six months of Esther's beauty treatments.[2] We know from Exodus 30:23 that myrrh is an ingredient of the holy anointing oil used by the priest. Myrrh was also one of the gifts the wise men brought to honor Jesus at His birth (Matt. 2:11) as well as what Nicodemus brought to honor Jesus at His death (John 19:39). Myrrh was present at the beginning and the end of His life. Medicinally, myrrh possesses healing qualities that help prevent infections and allow wounds to heal more quickly. Myrrh was used during embalming to mask the smell of death and decay. Its scent smells like Christmas—earthy pine tree undertones, a little hint of spicy and slightly smoky—taking us from the Old Testament to Bethlehem to the cross.

Olive oil also has healing properties. During biblical times it served many uses, from cooking to providing light to anointing. It is the oil referenced in the parable of the ten virgins who went out with their lamps to meet the bridegroom. The only way to produce olive oil is for the whole olive to be crushed. All parts of the olive's identity—pit, fruit, and skin—are subjected to the pressing. Removing one piece from the process will result in a product that does not bear the fullness of what is possible.

Trauma can leave you feeling fragmented—like your identity is in pieces. It can cause identity segmentation, leaving you feeling broken and detached. Have you ever battled impostor syndrome? Do you find it difficult to be intimate with your spouse? Do you wrestle with loneliness but find it impossible to put yourself out there to build friendships? It can feel like a part of you is refusing to come into agreement with you as a whole person. In the unveiling, the disconnected parts of your identity reconnect with your body, soul, and spirit. It's time to be whole again. All of you is subjected to a renewal process—the bitter and the sweet, the joy and the sorrow.

If Esther is like most of us, she had seen bitter moments in her life before the palace. And her life didn't become perfect when she became the queen. She was unveiled so that she could use her influence to save her people. You may recall her cousin's epic words: "For if you remain silent at this time, relief and deliverance for the Jews will arise from another place, but you and your father's family will perish. And who knows but that you have come to your royal position for such a time as this?" (Est. 4:14).

Insert your story into hers. Where have you been wounded by life? When has death and disease violated your peace? Metaphorically, God offers you His myrrh to ease the pain and usher in renewal. Bitterness must not remain a part of your identity. If left untended, it becomes a destructive root. It overtakes the good and drains the virtue out of everything in your life. This is one of the great rewards of becoming. As God uproots soul entanglements such as bitterness, envy, and pride, His Spirit sets you free from beliefs and attitudes you did not realize were holding you back.

This beautification process helps you see the end from the beginning. As you navigate bitter moments, you can see the joy set before you. Even when life feels too difficult to endure, the Lord pours out His oil. He pours without limits, covering every injury, every wound, every heartache, every injustice. Jesus covers them all. In Psalm 45:8, David says of the Lord, "All your robes are fragrant with myrrh and aloes and cassia." These are some of the same elements used during Esther's time of beautification. This process of cleansing, soaking, and crushing brings forth beauty from the pain and bitterness and releases a sweet aroma. We begin to smell like Jesus our King.

> Bitterness must not remain a part of your identity. If left untended, it becomes a destructive root. It overtakes the good and drains the virtue out of everything in your life.

The beautification process does not undo painful situations. Rather it allows you the space and the grace to process the effect those situations had on you. You discover what it did to your heart, your mind, and your spirit and reveal what needs to be redeemed. This time of preparation redirects your attention from the pain you've experienced to the good that can be resurrected from the pain. It's an opportunity to look to Jesus and behold Him as your Lord and King. As you truly behold Him, you will see a clearer reflection of yourself.

Like Esther, you have been set apart. Your life reflects the cross with periods of waiting, painful sacrifice, grave seasons, and moments when the stone is rolled out of your path. The struggle has not been for nothing. In the waiting, you have been prepared. Out of the darkness, you have been raised up. And now the path is clear to step into a season of promotion. Promotion in your level of intimacy with God. Promotion in the expression and use of your gifts. Promotion in your ability to love others. Promotion in your ability to love yourself. You may not feel ready for this promotion, but don't worry. You will not have to navigate this next phase alone. Your King is with you. You can confidently receive your crown and walk into the places where God is leading you, the places where you belong and have always belonged.

Take a moment to envision your crown as a daughter of the King. The traumas you've walked through are the peaks at the top. Like hands raised high, they stand at attention praising God for healing your wounds. A bouquet of surrendered yeses stretching toward the heavens. The band around the crown of your head is the foundation on which everything stands—Jesus. Each precious gem within the body of your crown is a memorial stone representing situations where God showed up on your behalf.

Will you accept your crown? Will you say "yes" to the healing He offers? By accepting your crown, you are declaring, "God, I am who You say I am. I want to receive Your healing. I make myself available to You. I want to embrace every piece of my identity. I want to be a new creation. I want to be made whole. I want to fully know You and be fully known." Allow yourself to receive the oil He pours out lavishly and receive a vision of yourself seated with Him in heavenly places. One who has permission to boldly approach the throne without apology. One who can dream, build, grow, and do all things with God.

Belonging in God's Favor

Psalm 84:11 — "For the LORD God is a sun and shield; the LORD bestows favor and honor; no good thing does he withhold from those whose walk is blameless."

Practical application — Seek to live an honorable life. You belong in God's promise to bestow favor and honor for those who walk in His ways. Believe that He withholds no good thing from you. He is the ultimate Source and can provide every resource you need.

Luke 2:52 — "And Jesus grew in wisdom and stature, and in favor with God and man."

Practical application — Follow Jesus' example of growth and development in all areas of life—spiritually, intellectually, physically, and socially. Invest in personal growth through prayer, study, exercise, and cultivating healthy relationships. Build your character. Let these virtues guide your interactions and decisions, knowing that they attract favor and a good reputation both in God's eyes and in the eyes of others.

Esther 2:17 — "Now the king was attracted to Esther more than to any of the other women, and she won his favor and approval more than any of the other virgins. So he set a royal crown on her head and made her queen instead of Vashti."

Practical application — Trust in God's providence and timing, knowing He can elevate you to positions of influence and favor in unexpected ways. Be diligent and faithful in whatever tasks or roles you are given and remain open to opportunities He may place before you.

Daily Unveiling

1. Where do you see yourself within Esther's story?

2. It takes a humble heart to undergo an extended time of preparation. How has God been preparing your heart?

3. Favor positions you for godly promotion. Pray this simple prayer: "God, prepare me for my next level of favor as I walk the path You have for me."

Visit www.davidccook.org/access or scan this QR code with the camera on your phone to watch Beholding Video No. 5.

Access code: known

Chapter 21

THE MINISTRY OF
THE OPEN DOOR

Walking down a bustling city street in a historical southern town, I was lost in thought staring at the architecture of the buildings and enjoying the window-shopping. Suddenly I noticed I was walking alone. My husband had stopped in front of a door I had not observed.

Its weathered baby blue paint was framed by gold markings and an antique handle. There was no sign on the door, but something about it was inviting. Curiosity got the better of us, and we decided to turn the handle. As we stepped through the threshold, we entered a cozy little French patisserie. The aroma of freshly brewed coffee and the yeasty goodness of warm baked goods overpowered my low-carb willpower. The chocolate croissants called my name. Settling at a table, we realized this unexpected detour had led us to a delightful new experience. It brought back fond memories of our trip to Paris when we were younger and reminded us of our desire for future adventures together. Isn't it amazing how a simple door can lead to so much more?

In John 10:9, Jesus declares, "I am the door. If anyone enters by me, he will be saved and will go in and out and find pasture" (ESV). Jesus describes Himself as the door through which we can enter and find abundant life. Through Him we gain access to a restored relationship with God the Father and all the blessings that flow from this reunion and covenant. Jesus became the door for us to experience forgiveness, grace, and eternal life.

Just as Jesus was the door for us, we can choose to be a door for others. We can open opportunities for them to discover something life-changing and wonderful. This is the ministry of the open door. When you step into your sacred work and find places of belonging, you will have access others do not have. Be a door. Give them access to the hope, healing, and wholeness you have found in Christ. There are people all around you who are hurting and in need of the Savior. God wants to use you to reach them with His love and lead them through the door of salvation, leading to deliverance and restoration.

The process of beholding, becoming, and belonging is God's gift to you and to the world. It redeems your past trauma, moves you past your spiritual fire walls, and places you in sacred spaces to be used by God. As you make yourself available to God, He will bring people across your path who need someone to open the door of faith and point them back to Jesus. Being a door for others will require intentionality, availability, and a willingness to be led by God. But there is no greater joy than being used by God to open the door for someone to encounter the living Christ. May we be faithful to swing wide the door of God's love and grace to those who desperately need it.

Divine Intervention

The busyness of life can interfere with our ability to find the Door and be a door. We have already talked about the sisters Mary and Martha. Mary sat at the feet of Jesus, enjoying time in His presence, soaking up His every word. Martha, on the other hand, rolled up her sleeves and set to work on the to-do list. I am an unapologetic Martha. Most of my closest friends are also Marthas. Workaholics tend to prefer to be around other workaholics. Those Mary types frustrate us. But regardless of your natural temperament, each of us has a Mary spirit inside that loves spending time with Jesus. We all crave moments when we can press up against His chest as the beloved.

We Marthas don't love God any less than the Marys in our lives. We just prefer expressing our love through service and activity. When I see pain or dysfunction in the world, I feel the Martha within me rising. I feel a call to action and am compelled to explore places I may not otherwise venture into. Territory is extended and boundaries are crossed for the sake of answering the call. But in my determination to serve well, I must be careful not to stray outside of God's best for me. I need to recall Psalm 46:10: "Be still, and know that I am God." I must remember that He is God and I am not.

Mary and Martha are two sides of the same human coin. Their story provides valuable insights into the dangers of toxic independence, the pitfalls of being a lone wolf, and the importance of burnout prevention. Martha busily prepares a meal for Jesus and His disciples while Mary sits at the Savior's feet, soaking in His teachings. When Martha complains to Jesus that Mary is not helping her, Jesus gently rebukes her, telling her that Mary has chosen the better thing. *Ouch!* He emphasizes the importance of prioritizing spiritual nourishment over physical tasks.

The story of these sisters highlights the risks of choosing doing over being. Like Martha, I have fallen into the trap of toxic independence, believing I must shoulder the responsibilities alone—that it's all up to me. I refused to delegate at work, fearing others would mess it up. In pride I have been unwilling to ask for help, even when I desperately needed it. This lone wolf mentality will lead to burnout as the demands of work and life become overwhelming. When you try to do everything yourself, you eventually run into your own limitations.

To prevent burnout and find harmony between doing and being, we must learn from Martha's divine intervention. As Jesus cautioned her, He cautions you too. Choose what is better, the thing that cannot be taken from you (Luke 10:42). Take time to sit at Jesus' feet and learn from Him. Prioritize rest and Sabbath-keeping. Set boundaries, delegate tasks, and seek support from others. By nurturing your own well-being and cultivating meaningful relationships, you can avoid the pitfalls of toxic independence and find the joy of being with Jesus and in community.

Jesus did not condemn work. Instead, He reminded Martha of the importance of beholding. He invited her to be a beholder. His words were a divine intervention to help her disengage from an identity of doing and engage with simply being.

Arise and Roam

Far too many of us have grown accustomed to going it alone. We excel in solitude but struggle to thrive in community. We each need both Marys and Marthas in our lives. We desire kinship with others who will champion our natural identities. Obtaining these types of relationships requires effort and the willingness to be the friend we desire. Authentic community provides a safe space to celebrate wins and praise reports without hesitation. A community where you can boldly declare, "Look what God did!" and your allies support the triumph. A community where you fearlessly rally around one another's God-given visions. And when the enemy tries to steal from you or lie to you, these friends have your back as you stand firm in truth and reclaim your family, children, and everything that is rightfully yours.

These are the ones cheering you on, saying, "Go, girl! I'm right here with you, praying you through to victory." Life-changing community is found in open-door circles of women who refuse to compete and instead complete each other. When you win, I win. We win together. For far too long, this door has been closed—overshadowed by ambition and positioning. It's time we reposition and put Christ back on the throne. Together we sit at His feet and receive. And together we can accomplish infinitely more than we ever could as individuals.

Lionesses instinctively understand the power of community. They roam as a pride for support, protection, and survival. The bond between lionesses exemplifies the strength found in unity. Each member of the pride plays a vital role. Whether in hunting, nurturing the young, or defending their territory, every talent is utilized. The lionesses lean on one another, sharing burdens and victories alike. Their interdependence speaks to our need for connection and belonging. Just as lionesses thrive in their pride, we, too, flourish when surrounded by a supportive community.

For years I have felt like a caged lioness. Each day, I paced back and forth behind the bars of my life, trapped by my concern about what others thought, stifled by societal pressures and people-pleasing. Just outside the cage, I could see the wide open spaces I longed to explore. But I felt confined by my limitations and circumstances. I feared freedom—the thing that would make me feel the most alive.

Freedom does not feel stable. There are no guardrails on which to prop your expectations. You must lay down your comfort to step into the unknown. It takes courage to go into wide open spaces with God—spaces where He is moving things, shifting your perspective, and orchestrating your steps. In these places you must surrender control. Leaving the comfortable confines of your self-imposed limitations is scary. But when you dare to step out with Him, you discover a freedom and purpose you never knew before.

The process of breaking free from your restrictions can lead you to forget your "lamb" side. Like Jesus, we carry the capacity to be both lion and lamb. Psalm 23 reminds us that we have a Shepherd. The Shepherd is the one who holds you and provides for you. You are never in a place of not having enough or not being enough because you are with the One who is more than enough. Maybe it's easier for you to embrace the lion side. You are willing to take hard steps of faith, show your strength, fight for your family. You're the one awake and praying in the middle of the night, storming the gates of heaven with tears streaming down your face.

You have endured much and carry wisdom and resilience forged in the fire. But your Good Shepherd wants to remind you it's also okay to be a lamb. It's okay to be vulnerable and to have needs. It's okay to share your softer side and to need the Shepherd. It's okay to take a moment to just recline, to stop worrying and thinking about all the things you have to do. It's okay to lean back against His chest and listen to His heartbeat. It's okay to roam beside the still waters and enjoy the green pastures. It's okay to be the sheep, the one who must be led, cared for, and protected.

> Embracing your lion boldness in tandem with your lamb vulnerability enables you to live with confidence and determination while also finding peace, provision, and comfort in His arms.

Part of being a child of God is embracing moments of dependence on your Good Shepherd. He doesn't ask you to be the strong one fighting the battles on your own. In fact, His Word says, "The LORD will fight for you; you need only to be still" (Ex. 14:14). Allow yourself to be restored and refreshed by His loving presence. Embracing your lion boldness in tandem with your lamb vulnerability enables you to live with confidence and determination while also finding peace, provision, and comfort in His arms. We are free to rise to every challenge and roam unrestricted. Dependence on God does not diminish your strength but rather allows you to be replenished and empowered to grow even stronger.

God doesn't ask you to be one thing or the other. Just as Jesus was both lion and lamb, you also possess qualities of both. You can be vulnerable and strong, sensitive and still powerful. Psalm 18:19 encourages us with this truth: "He brought me out into a spacious place; he rescued me because he delighted in me." His desire is not to keep you confined but to lead you into wide open places because He delights seeing you roam free. Reject the limitations and fears that have held you back. God is calling you to live in the fullness of all He created you to be. You are both lioness and lamb, beautifully and wonderfully made to reveal different aspects of God's nature to the world.

Open Doors

The ministry of the open door began with Jesus and finds its fullness in you. Reconciling your inner lioness and lamb in Him is the finished work of beholding, becoming, and belonging. You become an open door through which the Holy Spirit can flow, accomplishing His purposes. From this place, you roar your loudest roar undaunted by the reactions of those around you. You are an unstoppable force. The words of friendly attackers do not shake your faith or displace the identity God is unveiling. You know who you are, and you know *whose* you are. You are at peace with the fullness of your identity. You feel fully known in heaven and on earth.

You know how to run in a pack and collaborate with others, cheering on the person running beside you, even if she crosses the finish line first. You seek opportunities to open doors wide for others. You also know how to hunt alone. You are familiar with the secret place; you cherish intimacy and communion with the Father, Son, and Holy Spirit. You've discovered how to hunger for God's heart, how to rest in His presence, and how to find His peace in the middle of the unknown.

It is my prayer that each one of you becomes familiar with both the lioness inside of you as well as the lamb characteristics you possess. Both are needed. Both are necessary for being fully known and experiencing the joyful satisfaction of a Spirit-led life. In your being and your doing, may you find yourself in wide open places, perfectly loved, living a life above and beyond anything you ever imagined.

Belonging in God's Joy

Psalm 16:11 — "You make known to me the path of life; you will fill me with joy in your presence, with eternal pleasures at your right hand."

Practical application — Belonging in God's joy recognizes that true and lasting satisfaction is only found in His presence. Make it a priority to spend time daily in His presence. Cultivate a deep and intimate relationship with God. Allow His joy to fill every corner of your being.

John 15:11 — "I have told you this so that my joy may be in you and that your joy may be complete."

Practical application — Belonging in God's joy involves accepting His invitation to share in His joy completely. Align your heart with His purposes. Abide in His love by allowing His joy to permeate the work you do and bring completeness. Listen to the still, small voice of

His Spirit and respond. Attune your ear to heaven, knowing that true satisfaction is found in God alone.

1 Peter 1:8–9 — "Though you have not seen him, you love him; and even though you do not see him now, you believe in him and are filled with an inexpressible and glorious joy, for you are receiving the end result of your faith, the salvation of your souls."

Practical application — Belonging in God's joy releases an authentic expression that comes from knowing Him. Embrace both your spiritual and natural identity—the joy of your salvation and the joy of using your gifts and talents for His purposes. Let His joy fill your heart and overflow into your sacred work. Be a door for others by bearing witness to the transformative power of beholding God's love, mercy, comfort, power, and grace. Remember, He was beholding you long before you started beholding Him.

Daily Unveiling

1. Who do you most identify with—Martha or Mary? Lioness or lamb?
2. What do you believe to be the pros and cons of each of these four identities?
3. Jesus is both lion and lamb. As His image-bearer, so are you. Pray this simple prayer of gratitude: "God, because of You, I can be fully known. Thank you."

21-Day Fasting Guide

Fasting is a spiritual practice to help you become more aware of God's presence in your life. This twenty-one-day fasting plan accompanies *Being Fully Known*—which consists of twenty-one chapters. Each day, you will focus on a specific chapter while engaging in a time of fasting and prayer.

Types of fasts

1. Full Fast: Abstain from all food and consume only water or clear liquids. (This type of fast is typically done for shorter periods up to twenty-four to thirty-six hours.)
2. Partial Fast: Eliminate certain foods or eat at specified times of day only.
3. Daniel Fast: Eat only fruits, vegetables, and water; no meat, dairy, or processed foods.
4. Media Fast: Abstain from social media, television, or other forms of entertainment.

Preparing for your fast

1. If you have health concerns or conditions, consult your doctor prior to beginning any type of fast.
2. Choose the type of fast that best suits your physical and spiritual needs.
3. Make a plan and gather necessary supplies: plan meals, remove apps from your phone or other devices, etc.

4. Set aside dedicated time each day for prayer, reading, and reflection.

Daily fasting guide

1. Pray before you begin reading each day, asking God to make Himself known to you.

2. Read the corresponding day's chapter from *Being Fully Known*. (Example: On the first day of your fast, you will read chapter 1 of the book.)

3. Reflect on the chapter's content and how it applies to your life.

4. Spend time in personal prayer, focusing on the theme and lessons from the chapter.

5. Write down your thoughts, insights, and revelations from that day's Daily Unveiling.

6. Follow your chosen fast, staying attentive to God's presence within your day and how He is speaking to you.

7. At the end of each day, thank the Lord for His faithfulness and the work He's doing in your life.

Breaking your fast

1. After twenty-one days, reintroduce normal foods gradually.

2. Keep your schedule with God, continuing the beholding, becoming, and belonging activities you cultivated during your fast.

3. Share what you're learning with family members and friends and encourage them to lean in to being known by God from wherever they are in their journey.

Keep in mind that the purpose of this fast is to deepen your relationship with God and allow Him to work in your life. As you commit to twenty-one days of *Being Fully Known*, trust God to reveal Himself to you in new ways and enable you to experience the joy and satisfaction of beholding, becoming, and belonging.

ABOUT THE AUTHOR

Dr. Saundra Dalton-Smith is an internal medicine physician and host of *I Choose My Best Life* podcast where she encourages listeners to live fully, love boldly, and rest intentionally. She is the author of numerous books including bestsellers *Sacred Rest: Recover Your Life, Renew Your Energy, Restore Your Sanity*, and *Set Free to Live Free: Breaking Through the 7 Lies Women Tell Themselves.*

Dr. Saundra is an international speaker, communicating with audiences on the topics of overcoming limiting beliefs, purposeful living, and finding restorative rest. Through heartfelt stories and biblical truths, she loves to share God's Word at retreats, conferences, and ministry events. You can invite her to speak by sending an email to support@DrDaltonSmith.com.

Connect with Dr. Saundra:

Instagram: www.instagram.com/drdaltonsmith

Facebook: www.facebook.com/DrSaundraDaltonSmith

Podcast: https://ichoosemybestlife.libsyn.com/

YouTube: www.youtube.com/@SaundraDaltonSmith

ACKNOWLEDGMENTS

Every book I've written is a collaborative work filled with my stories and the experiences of those I've had the pleasure of doing life with. Thank you to all the women who have joined me within my membership and mastermind groups. Your transparency and authenticity were the catalyst for this book. Your realness encourages me.

My long hours at the computer are a sacrifice my family has endured without complaint. I am grateful to my husband, Bobby, and our sons, Tristan and Isaiah. You guys are my biggest supporters. Your love energizes every word. This book is another memorial stone of God's faithfulness in our family. I behold Him daily when I look at each of you.

Sheryl and Heidi, you are the sisters I didn't know I needed. After years of trying to do everything on my own, God graced my life with you two. Our monthly calls and Bible study time have been an anchor in my life. To my pastors, Kent and Bev Mattox, and my prayer team, Perdeta, Barb, Suzan, and Becky, your daily intercessions for me and my family are an invaluable blessing. Thank you for your regular check-ins and prayer coverage.

Bob Hostetler and Steve Laube, you are a power duo and your guidance in my writing career has been unmatched. My heartfelt thanks also go to the team at David C Cook and Esther Press. Your creativity, professionalism, and commitment to excellence are truly inspiring.

To you, the readers, who have joined me on this journey—thank you for your curiosity, your openness, and your desire to be fully known. I pray these words will resonate with you, reverberate through you, and inspire you to open doors through both your being and doing.

NOTES

Chapter 6

1. Search Institute, "Develomental Assets Framework," https://searchinstitute.org/resources-hub/developmental-assets-framework, accessed Nov. 15, 2024.

2. Steven L. Berman et al., "Trauma and identity: A reciprocal relationship?" *Journal of Adolescence* 79, no. 1 (2020): 275–78.

Chapter 8

1. Biblegateway, s.v. "El Shaddai, El Shadday," www.biblegateway.com/resources/encyclopedia-of-the-bible/El-Shaddai-El-Shadday, accessed Nov. 15, 2024

Chapter 9

1. Beatcrave, "The Meaning Behind The Song: The Little Drummer Boy (Carol of the Drum); carol by Erich Kunzel, https://beatcrave .com/the-meaning-behind-the-song-the-little-drummer-boy-carol -of-the-drum-carol-by-erich-kunzel/#The_Meaning_Behind_The _Song_The_Little_Drummer_Boy_Carol_of_the_Drum, Nov. 8, 2023.

Chapter 17

1. W. Smith, "Anointing," *Smith's Bible Dictionary*, revised ed., (Nashville: Thomas Nelson, 2004).

Chapter 20

1. David Guzik, "Esther 2–Esther is Chosen Queen", *The Enduring Word Bible Commentary*, https://enduringword.com/bible -commentary/esther-2/, accessed Nov. 15, 2024..

2. Hope Bolinger, "What Does the Bible Say About Anointing Oil and it's Importance?", www.biblestudytools.com/bible-study/topical -studies/why-is-anointing-oil-important-in-the-bible.html, Aug. 5, 2024.

DAVID C COOK

JOIN US.
SPREAD THE GOSPEL.
CHANGE THE WORLD.

We believe in equipping the local church with Christ-centered resources that empower believers, even in the most challenging places on earth.

We trust that God is *always* at work, in the power of Jesus and the presence of the Holy Spirit, inviting people into relationship with Him.

We are committed to spreading the gospel throughout the world—across villages, cities, and nations. We trust that the Word of God will transform lives and communities by bringing light to the darkness.

As a global ministry with a 150-year legacy, David C Cook is dedicated to this mission. Each time you purchase a resource or donate, you're supporting a ministry—helping spread the gospel, disciple believers, and raise up leaders in some of the world's most underserved regions.

Your support fuels this mission.
Your partnership sends the gospel where it's needed most.

Discover more. Be the difference.
Visit DavidCCook.org/Donate